Get your own...

Money Genies!

-Learn to invoke & earn 24x7!

SRINIVAS BANGALORE THIRUNAVAKKARASU

Copyright © Srinivas Bangalore Thirunavakkarasu 2021

No part of this book may be reproduced or transmitted in any form or means whatsoever, either electronic, or physical, or mechanical, including photocopying, recording, or by any informational storage or retrieval system without the written, dated, and signed permission from the author.

DISCLAIMER OF WARRANTY

The author and publisher of this book have used their best effort in preparing the content of this book. The author or publisher makes no representation or warranties concerning any of the content directly, implied, or derived. All the names of individuals, companies, products, services, or any kind of naming are fictional and the author claims no responsibility and does not represent any of them, or their opinions even if they are real coincidentally. The author and the publisher disclaim any warranties, expressed or implied, and merchantability for any purpose whatsoever. The author and publisher shall in no event be held liable for any loss or other damages, including but not limited to special, incidental, consequential, or other damages. The information contained in this publication is compiled and presented solely from the understanding of the author on the same, and the author assumes no responsibility for error or omissions. The information and strategies contained in this publication are not intended to constitute or replace or substitute professional advice. The plans, strategies, and suggestions in this publication may not be suitable for every individual, are not meant to provide general or individualized recommendations or advice.

To the

Omnipresent, Omnipotent, Almighty!

&

My Parents

Bhavani B. T. and Thirunavakkarasu A. S.

Contents

Preface

As busy professional, working for over 20 years now, I realized many of the stresses people go through and discuss, as if it is inevitable and very much part of life, is not right. There are many who go through life with ease and pleasure no matter what happens. Basically, for a busy professional Monday Blues and "Thank God It's Friday" are accepted as very normal experiences. This is challenged by many, either knowingly or unknowingly and live a life of fulfillment and abundance.

When I finally realized this, did study and understood how many have live wonderfully, some without even going through TGIF kind of experiences, and others have got through it after having realized, how easy it is to do that, especially in this era of ubiquitous internet.

Many are driven so deep into to the crevices of corporate world that it pushes their health and relationships to irreparable levels. Having seen both of these close enough, and studied them, I wrote this book to bring awareness and show clearly, how living a life of abundance time and money is very much possible.

It might not be easy, but It is very much possible and there are 100s of true-life stories all around us. I have worked as a software engineer for almost 2 decades and having seen the growth of internet and the companies based on them, there is a clear picture of how people have made it.

Having started on the path for some time now, I see this trend is picking up all over the globe. I have put together the most required reasoning, the "Why", for having to leverage technology to work for you. All the Engineering innovations has just one main purpose, make human and in general life efficient, convenient. That is the only purpose of any machine, to enhance the experience of life. We should make sure, it serves that purpose instead of losing out on time, to a lower extent than olden days, when there were no machines.

We have become so busy in making machines, or running after "made up luxuries and egos", that we are working for machines, rather than they work for us.

There are many, who have already achieved the dream life of this era, leveraging technology, and the best part is not all of them were engineers or techies or born rich or born highly talented. The machines work for anyone who learns how to use them. I have put down my observation, understandings and learning from many who have been generous enough to share, how they did it. It just takes the intent and willingness to take action.

It's time to set the right priorities and leverage!

Acknowledgments

I thank the Almighty God, making me the person I am, and for all the gifts I am receiving…

I express my deepest gratitude and thanks,

To my Parents Bhavani and Thirunavukkarasu for the unconditional support all through life.

To my Late. Grandmother Rajeshwari Ammal, who took pride in everything I did.

To my Late. Grandfather Seeyalam and Late. Uncle Appadurai and Ganesh, for making my childhood such a beautiful experience!

To my sisters Lakshmi & Priyadarshini who are pillars of my strength.

To my wife Savitha Lakshmi, and daughters Riya and Isha who are my source of inspiration.

My heartiest gratitude to Irfan Noorani and Arfeen Khan for the mastermind and guidance in writing this book. The constant follow-up and motivation with the group were just amazing, in fact, the entire reason I could finish writing this book.

My salute, gratitude, and thanks to all the Gurus, starting from Srila Prabhupada, who I have been following for more than 3 decades.

So many other Gurus and influencers who I have been following and learning from, almost all using virtual technology and books, for many years now, Sadhguru Jaggi Vasudev, Osho, Sarvapriananda.

Introduction

Once you read this book

At the Least

You will have answers for the questions below,

At the Best

6 months after reading and acting, people will see that you know it for sure!

1. How do I make all the money I want?
2. How to make extra income, using free time?
3. Can I make money working anytime I want to?
4. How do I make money work for me?
5. Will I be able to ever get out of 9-5 job?
6. How do I make my business work for me?
7. How will I have the vacations I always wanted?
8. Will I still have the job after 5 years from now?
9. How will I survive if I lose my job?
10. How do I provide for my family without a corporate job?
11. Should I be Lucky, Born Rich, or a Techie to earn money using technology?
12. Are all the Internet Millionaires Engineers or Technical masters?

1. Earning meaningful money

What is meaningful money? why you should build a secondary source of income? The first reason, everything is changing rapidly, there are newer skills being developed and being used in various fields and areas of work, and you have to adopt to the new changes, as life takes keeps moving you ahead all the time. No matter who you are it's always forward, that life takes you.

If you look at it carefully, it is very clear that change is the only thing that is constant, no matter which time you live in. There has always been change and it continue to be so. So, you cannot keep doing the same thing, whatever you were doing earlier, and hope that your profession will stay, and you will be able to make an income out of it, and a living out of it. You will be in real trouble if you realize this at a later point in time.

Now, if you remember earlier things which were happening in India where the train reservation employees or the bank transaction employees or the construction workers used to work. For rail reservations there used to be a huge queue and people trying to get the ticket booked, racing against the clock and constantly checking which queue if moving faster, it used to be like India Pakistan cricket match!

Myself or anyone for that matter, unaware of what computer and its network could do, would easily and always think there was huge scope to add more counter employees. That job they held looked to go on for a long time. The demand seemed to be high. We now know what really has happened to all of that. The innovations in computers and networking changed the complete scenario. It can be done 24 hours a day, the transactions are totally done by the machines.

Similar changes for the construction workers which they used to take months, also resulting in employment of 100s. Now digging up, mixing the concrete, carrying it over to the ceiling, and all the related activities are replaced to very great extent by huge machines. Hundreds of workers got replaced, it's not bad that they are getting replaced, from one perspective that, it has eliminated any human being to do such physically straining and risky work. At the same time, the major concern is, do all those workers have a means for livelihood now. Though the risk of injury and to their lives is reduced, how good are they surviving?

This clearly shows you have to move with the times, and times are changing rapidly, so watch out for the newer skills that will be required and develop and them. You should keep on developing and keep on watch, you should be able to generate income from the other skill, you have to contribute to your thriving money and abundant money pull, not just for looking for the surviving money. You should not be focusing just on the "now", you should be focusing on the short term and also the long term. You should focus on the thriving money, and abundant money, do not take anything for granted.

As and when there are new professions are getting created, you should be able to leverage that to your advantage, or the other best thing you could do is whatever you have learned, try to maximize the gains out of it, just by disassociating your time from the job. Also, try to extend the service which you can render beyond your physical presence using technology. Technology it the greatest gift mankind has received, in fact created for itself.

Remember you can do so many things, with technology available to you, and is so affordable compared to the value it provides, I can't just stop wondering. You could just talk to anyone looking at them and their environment as if they are standing next to you. You are in night, on one side of the globe, and can talk to a person standing in daylight! Look at the Sun, while you are in night. You can address and talk to 1000s of people all over the globe at the same time! Just imagine this kind of power was not available even to the greatest Kings and Emperors who walked this Planet ever!

Still, you are thinking you need to be physically present to render a service!?

Just make sure you are good at what you are doing, rest technology will do it for you!

Now, if you are either in a nine to five job, or in a small business requiring straight forward "Trade your time for money", it's time to reflect. Not that it is bad, but just that you are just being a spectator to greatest gifts any kind of life form has ever received in all of history, while you could be a very big part of it, and the best part, it's just very easy to do so. The only thing standing in between, is your own beliefs or self-imposed limitations.

You should avoid time trade to earn money, this is the riskiest thing to do, but usually this is the only way you can start doing any work, or learn anything, get experience, build your skill and start making your living. So, this is very much essential, but you should make sure that you do not make this as your only source of income, all the time. To start with, it is a good thing, but it will not be the one which will help you to thrive and to be able to survive in the long term, especially when there are some immediate or big requirement for money, all of a sudden you will have really consumed or destroyed all your savings one shot and you will not be able to do any other activity.

With 9-5 jobs, and small businesses the only way to increase the amount of money you earn is by increasing the amount of time spent on the particular work. Looking at the way how you got to this place, basically it will be something similar to this. You studied for around the 15-16 years without a break, making sure your work all throughout, at least inconsistently, studying, doing all the required assignments, preparing and clear all the tests, learning newer skills testing them out, and making sure it is at least on par with your peers, if not trying to exceed them. Then, you get out in search of a job or prepare with lot of effort during your studies and after one or a lot of interviews you make you entry into your dream company. Now, will they start paying, just because of all the efforts (more than one and half decade of it!) No! not yet dear, you have to work for a month.

Voila! Great! Now you got you first pay! That's a fantastic news, enjoy!

The only small catch is, you have to repeat the work, with all what you have learnt, every month till you need the pay! Very simple… Of course, there is another very small catch, whatever you have learnt till now has got you thus far, still you need to continue doing that to make sure you keep going and able to at least match the inflation in the country.

You have to gain experience acquire additional skills, and make sure your skills are at par with the market, not just the academic knowledge what you have gained, but you should be making sure all the time that you are on par with the market, and the newer innovations which are always being pumped into the market. Also, you have to keep up with the newer people getting added to the industry every year. Many a times you will just go and acquire a master's degree in the same technology or in the same business area or service area for the betterment of your job and to get a higher paying job, to account for your higher expenses, or the inflation at the least. This keeps happening in an incremental way.

Now, think about it, can you really repeat this, if the profession changes, or the technology changes drastically, which is very likely to happen at some point in time or the other.   For instance, you were doing design and architecture drawing huge plans, and now software came up with much easier way to do the same and print out the whole thing, you could either learn the software with a little bit change in area of your work, and try to survive or acquire the next level of skills at this time not easily replaceable by machines and make the transition as soon as possible and start thriving again or you will just barely survive for however long possible.

If you look at it, things can change so drastically that all you have learned over 16 to 18 years might be almost obsolete. You can't repeat the whole learning process all over again. So, you should be doing one of these, simple first step:

1. Increase your income by leveraging your skill, by operating at the next level, leading a team to multiply the outcome and there by multiplying your income. This is not possible in all the professions, then you should look at the other option of increasing your income.
2. Build a secondary source of income, using the same skill which you have acquired with so much effort, to make sure you leverage it to the maximum, and able to earn the maximum. This will contribute to your thriving and abundant money corpus. How to do this, we will look at in detail.

Now, if you are in a small business, either self-built or inherited, there will be same kind of time trade and requirement to multiply the income.

The small business is quite different from the bigger businesses where the process and people will be forced to take care of 80% of the required activities. Small business is as good as a 9-5 job because you have to spend all the time, constantly monitoring or providing the service, and be able to earn money. Big corporations will be totally independent of the person who has started it or owns it. It is a system where a lot of people are there with a lot of processes in place, which take care of all operations including profit making and expansion. You as an owner of it, could monitor with very less time and very less physical presence, these are usually the companies which employ more than 500 employees.

The small businesses are usually family owned and inherited ones or established by a person based directly on current market needs. The businesses would be in a particular area or niche. There are lot of factors that might affect these either favourably or adversely, such as, Government policy changes or Technology disruptions, and events such as conflicts or pandemics.

Once again, you will not be able to repeat the whole process of how you established or inherited the business. The only thing that could rescue is the asset, if you have created when the business was thriving, by moving into another one. You have to make sure whatever skill you have learned, and whatever your business is built on, is leveraged to the maximum, by generating additional or increased income to contribute to your Thriving and Abundant money pools and keep yourself safe and insured (while you still have life!).

We will look at how to really leverage the skill or business you already have to make your Thriving and Abundant money pools.

Types of money

We will look clearly at the importance of earning money, especially earning meaningful money while you start off your career and progress through it. The first thing we have to understand is, what is meaningful money?

It is basically a combination of three kinds of money for an individual, from the perspective of what it takes care of. Which are:

1. Immediate money.
2. Surviving money.
3. Thriving and Abundant money.

Immediate money is the one which is required to have the survival going through and pay all the bills. This basically takes care of your monthly expenses.

Surviving money is the amount of money which, if you have, will be able take care of a year of all your living expenses, without requiring to change your current life style. You will be able to carry on without having to worry about working a day for one complete year.

Thriving and Abundant money is the amount of money which can take care of you for a complete decade. This basically has the ability to easily keep you and your family going for a decade, answering all contingencies. Now, why just a decade, not 50 years? This is to make sure you are having a meaningful target and you don't end up spending earning this kind of money all your life. Looking back, you see you have a Thriving and Abundant money built, but have lost all the prime time in your life. Once you have a decade's worth of buffer built, you can get the money earn money. This will keep you going as long as you want, you have to just make sure, you keep a tab on it.

Earning meaningful money

There are lot of options such as stocks, real estate assets, brand building, etc. which we will explore and understand in the coming chapters. You will be able to really multiply and will never have to linearly trade your time for money ever again. This is more like an investment principle, which will take care of all your expenses and you can just focus on whatever your passion is, or whatever you love to do all the time. Whatever you are doing you should always be thinking of these three pools of money the ISTAM (Immediate, Surviving, Thriving Abundant Money)

This is not magic or a damn new concept, many have achieved it either consciously or otherwise. The ones who do this consciously are the ones, who do not go back to square one, make sure to achieve Abundance state and stay there. Make sure you are one of them! Statistics show, it is just 3% of the world population who reach and sustain this!

But now comes the question of what happens to people when they really start earning some money. After having learned some skill, or having studied in school and colleges for quite a number of years, and ultimately succeeding in getting a job, either immediately after college or after a little bit of struggle. They begin to work, especially in a nine to five job, or in a small business, they start up very well in terms they are able to take care of the immediate money. After maybe say five years or four years down the lane, they will be able to get good money also. That is, able to provide for a year, but only a miniscule percentage of these people really end up making the Thriving Abundant money, which will take care of them 40 or 50 years ahead. These are the ones who can really work on their passion, which is, really what they want to work all life.

Why does this happen? It happens because of the general way how the whole society is built up, at least that is the way it is easily perceived. Once you get into a nine to five job or small business, where you trade your time for earning money. Though this initially works properly, but after some time you will find that you will not be able to increase your working hours just to increase the amount of money you're earning, there are just 24 hours a day so if you are making X amount of money working 8 hours a day, and if you want to make 4x of that amount, will you be able to work 32 hours every day?

It is not possible to do this time trade all the time, but people just forget about this, or don't realize this, especially in this era where you have a lot of loans available. Add to it there are lot of people trying to engage you in those loans with various kinds of misleading things like:

❖ High projected Appreciation values. *
❖ Government benefits in terms of taxes. *
❖ Attractive initial Interests from banks. *
❖ High encouragement to enjoy expensive lifestyle! *

*Hidden cost = Your future.

You have promise to pay at least double the money you have borrowed, worst of all, this means you are promising to work 50% of your time, earning money for them.

Just realising this will make sure you are not giving in for immediate pleasures, making some purely emotional decision by getting into wrong assets. You will really lose all the leverage you could get. You will end up working for money all your life, instead of having the opportunity where money starts to work for you at the earliest. Surprisingly for some people it never works for them.

Happy pitfalls

Pitfalls every new employee or small business owners happily jump into!

Now we will see the various pitfalls, which new employees or the small business owners, happily jump into. We have seen that if you don't acquire the newer skills, or leverage the skills which you have already acquired or small business to generate a large amount of money, you will be in big trouble. You have to contribute to your own TAM (Thriving Abundant Money).

[On a lighter note, this will take care of your TAM (Total Address-able Market of your Lift-time) in terms of Available Free Time in your Life]

We will take some more examples now to see how things really change. We just saw the employee level changes like the ones that changed, reservation counters operated by human beings, the construction workers. If you look at the big things that are changing drastically, you will be able to clearly remember companies like Kodak, which used to manufacture cameras, photo films, have almost completely vanished, because they didn't adapt to the new trends and technologies. They in fact had the digital photography technology developed in-house, but were reluctant to move to it, afraid of losing out their own camera and films business.

The other very big example is the blockbuster company, which used to be the biggest DVD rental company in the world, which has been totally replaced by Netflix.

If you look at Facebook and Google, they have made billions of dollars not millions, billions of dollars, making the biggest and century old industrial companies look smaller. Those are the ones which manufactured tangible products. Companies like Tesla and Amazon are doing it so big and so fast, and they have become kind of super powerful. Some of these companies are more powerful than some countries. You can imagine how much of disruption is happening because of the technology. You cannot just sit down for any reason, thinking that whatever you're doing, will be there for long term. The pace in which changes are happening is also increasing. This is an accelerated change in the recent times. For instance, it took a lot of time to invent a phone, and from phone to mobile. Then, from mobile to smart phone was much faster. If you remember the way pager came in between and vanished, many of the millennials wouldn't even know a thing like pager ever existed and the use case of it!

You have to realize what change is happening in your work area or that of your interest very early and be able to make the changes and leverage it to your advantage, rather than losing out and becoming a victim of the whole thing.

Now, look at the pitfalls of new employee or small business owners. As soon as anyone starts with a new job, what they do is they get the same things they have a lot more money than what they used to have in the student times, so they start spending on small things and then they get into some usual gimmicks, played by the big companies, or the government or the industrial nature of the whole setup, which actually works all the time, and pulling them into illusionary investments which are actually expenditures in disguise of an investment. The other easy trap is, looking at what the majority of people similar to you are doing.

Whenever you are on the side of the majority, It is time to pause and reflect.
-Mark Twain

You should be careful not to get into these common pitfalls, you should make sure that you understand and remember the three main pools of money which you have to build for yourself.

No one will build it for you. You have to build your own ISTAM.

One fantastic example we can look at and understand what kind of magic is possible if you really understand and take action on this. There was a person who started after his schooling, started working in an oil company overseas. Of course, he was good at whatever he was doing and started with this 9-5 job. Now, comes the most important part where he quickly realized how this is not very scalable and not conducive to increase contributions exponentially. So, he decided to leave that behind to start on his own. He was offered a higher pay to continue there, one of the common enticements, but he was clear, really clear on what the limitation was, so didn't accept. He wouldn't accept anything smaller than what he thought of. He started on his own ventures, from Silk, Trading, and finally oil. He was basically successful in any of the venture he started and set an example for a whole Nation.

Though he started making good money as an employee, but still, after some time he clearly realized that he is in a pit, or he is falling into a pit, and was able to realize that, and in spite of his employer offering him higher compensation, he did not accept it. He understood nothing could really compensate for his time. You should have already realized who I am talking about… it's none other than Mr. Dhirubhai Ambani.

He also gotten himself in a pitfall, but was quick enough to recognize that he was in one. Not only he realized, but took action to get out of it successfully, and came out with such colours, which inspires generations. So, the first thing to understand is that no one can help you, if you do not realize you are in a trouble.

**"I freed a thousand slaves.
I could have freed a thousand more if only they knew they were slaves."**

-Harriet Tubman.

For many, it is not a trap to begin with. This is the way you have to begin, but after some point in time this begins to be a limitation. If you keep continuing the same time-trade for money, whether you realize it or not, the places you can go will be seriously limited. This is like using a bicycle to commute as a child when you began. This is really good at that time to go around and might be to your school and around your city. Now, if you mistake it to be the only way you can commute or travel, the places you could go and the effort required will be quite different. Any 9-5 or Small business is like a bicycle, really good to get started. It's always better to find out and switch to the next level ones, to live your life fully.

Especially as you age (anybody and everybody does! Pls. don't mention the Yogi who is not aging!), you should use better means and methods leveraging on what you have already gained. Use bike, car, locomotive, a plane! Best part of it, as it goes in the analogy, you don't have to really own the method or process to use it!

Come on folks! How better can it get! Finish reading this book you will surely get started on the right path. There are a lot of books, of course I have devoured many of them, and putting my own experiences and the ones which I have witnessed first-hand in this book.

We will look at some more examples, first some of the small businesses which were established and seem to be going on forever or will go on forever, and have disappeared, one of them was the PCO and public telephone booths, which people used to make calls. With the advent of mobile phones and technology making them so very affordable, all those phone booths are totally gone. Similar thing happened to the small rental car companies. With the new business model immensely enabled by technology Uber, Ola, kind of companies came up at global scale and higher quality and reliability and accountability of service. With these newer companies anybody could experience the same kind of service which ever city they go. They could use the royalty points earned to book free rides! It's a huge leap in customer experience, which can't be matched by the small business owners.

This made those small business obsolete. Drivers are directly contracted by the big companies. Many of those business owners have transitioned to the newer model by engaging with the big companies, by renting out their cars. Of course, this is possible for those who had their Surviving Money or TAM ready!

If any small business owner with car rentals just totally relied upon the local solution, and didn't really build the money pools, he or she would be totally destroyed, or at least have a huge dip in life style and getting back up on track making a living.

This kind of changes not just doesn't affect small businesses, if you remember what happened to big shopping companies and malls like JCPenney, Sears, they are on the verge of filing bankruptcy. This is direct impact of the disruption caused by eCommerce with a global reach and enhanced customer experience and convenience. The kind of drastic changes in technology and the amount of flexibility they provide is really mind blowing. Even the big business owners were affected just because they didn't adapt to the newer trend. You cannot sit down there keep complaining or hoping changes will not happen or not happen fast enough. Keep abreast with latest technological and business model advances, and with your STAM built, you will be happily ready for any eventuality.

Starting a business without experience or proper research.

Now we'll see what happens when a person starts a business or a new adventure without having properly done the research or having the right experience. One of the very common first business adventure anyone plans is a Restaurant!

This is such a common thing that everyone gets an idea for it, because they see how easy it is, they are able to see the money coming in flowing into the cashier and into the restaurant but they don't see the full picture of what is really happening. This is where I also have a first-hand experience with my friend. This adventure was based on the available free time to establish another source of income, if you look at it, this was just for the purpose of earning money based on passion without proper vision. Obviously, the same way as majority of people gets started with.

Just looking at it from a user's perspective or whenever you are using it, you will feel as if money is flowing very rapidly and constantly, morning, afternoon and night. You will feel that there is a lot of money in the restaurant business. What you really miss is this is one of the most demanding business, and requiring its own set of skills. It might not require very high skills but whatever skills being used, it has to be done with utmost care. It has all other requirements of customer satisfaction, necessity of repeat customers, word of mouth marketing, unique selling point (USP), etc.

Now all this with the lowest shelf life of products, which you produce, the scale of employee attrition and need to maintain consistency both in quality and taste, sourcing of raw materials of required quality and price, you are really up against a very dynamic business. So, you cannot just get into a business without knowing the whole details of operation, and also the details of marketing, sales, and demand.

There are clearly different scales in which the restaurants operate. Almost everything from the products, the menu the design, the products, the employee recruitment, the maintenance of the quality the acquisition of the customers, repeat customers, shelf life of the products, way to deal with the raw materials, managing the whole show with supervisors, cooks, helpers, cleaners, security, cashiers. Everything is different from the bigger restaurants, which have a totally different operation and totally different way of doing things.

From the first-hand experience, the way it started with my friend deciding to use the free time, which is basically the weekends, and the late evenings. Now, as anyone usually think of logically, starting up a business, it started with research of the restaurants around. Checking out their operating methods, arriving at the menu, then getting a location to start up.

The location found was really good at it was a corner building, having a good elevation overlooking the road, with steps leading up to the front door of the shop. There was some buffer area in front of the shop until the road or payments started. This was a very good place for people to use all the open space and having a good view. It looked perfect and was booked.

Now, the menu was finalized and the next logical thing was to get the equipment for the restaurant. Straight, the search for equipment started online and using the phone dial up index, which is also available online started. There were various equipment manufacturers and vendors found. A list was made according to the menu, such as one burner style stoves, two burner stoves, tandoor (Arabian stove), a big Tawa (for Dosa and Rotis, the Indian pan cakes and breads), etc.

Went ahead to get the quotes from around 6 vendors, and after having compared the prices, it was all booked. Then came the furniture, basically the chair, dining tables, etc. which were also sourced in a very similar way. All brand-new equipment ready and the location fixed and booked. Just remember, all this is happening in the free time. Around three months of research and activity it's ready.

Now came the time to recruit the cooks, cleaners, etc. This started with putting out ads, and also scanning through the existing ones. To the surprise there are a lot of brokers or agents who really provide, the kind of people or the employees, including cooks the helpers, the cleaners, the supervisors and the cashiers. Also, each of the cuisines has their own set of cooks, assistant, helper, this was a learning at that point.

One cook was hired directly and the rest were from the agent. Then the business started with south Indian cuisine. This industry has a very high attrition and people keep on jumping one place to the other. Every month once the salary is paid, the next day you simply do not know whether they are going to come back for work or not. So, having an agent for the workforce is very handy.

With all this done, we had to find a way to get the word out about restaurant, in an emphatic manner to increase the sales. We found an innovative way, at least that was the opinion, by doing a one-day drastic discounted sale of 80%. Then after having discussion, it was decided to run it with 70%.

Printed pamphlets and distributed all over the place in the surroundings. This really worked out great in getting the word out and lot of people who turned up on the morning. Once this happened, everything was fine sales were good to start with. The offer day required lot of resources and people, and even the agent gave a helping on that day. After few days of this, the footfalls came down, which is natural as learnt from our own experience and reiterated by the agent. Initially what happens is the number of people who come are out of curiosity about the new restaurant. It's part of trying out newer things on weekends or on the weekdays whenever they have time. So, your customer base will be settling down around 30 to 50% of what happens in the first month.

Now we started looking closely at the amount of money flowing in from sales and how it is covering the initial capital, and the working capital. Soon it was realized that this is not going to work out had we had to expand. Expansion of menu was the way to attract lot more people, it was decided. Though Tandoor (the Arabian stove) was already bought, it was wasn't started just for the sheer volume required to make sure it gives ROI (return on investment) each day.

Anyway, north Indian cuisine, along with chats (evening snacks) were started after recruiting using the agent. This required a fresh inflow of capital, which came straight from our pockets, which were fast getting lighter!

There went another set of pamphlets, but with no discount, just the newer and updated menu. People were really interested and they tried again, a lot of people came in it seemed to have worked. Soon enough the same cycle repeated with declining walk-ins and orders. This time the effect from your initial capital drain also started showing effects. It became tougher to maintain with lot more cooks, assistants, helpers, etc. Now came in another surprise of internal conflicts, wow! Which had to be resolved then and there. All this happening on our "free time". So, not just the sales and marketing are the question but also internal management required proper attention.

Now, resorting to the great idea of CCTVs to be able to monitor and manage came in! There came the installation of them. If you have observed this just went into fire-fighting mode on free time. There were lot of discussions amongst us and also getting inputs from the Agent and others in the field, just drastically enhancing the clarity of what it really takes to make a restaurant successful.

We took out time, to really check if this is going to work the way it is being done. Clearly this wasn't going to work on the "free time". The scale and the approach both had to be different for establishing restaurant on "free time". Once this was clear and the restaurant was closed, one fine day!

After having gone through this whole experience there are precious learnings, which now could be clearly used to start-up, whenever required!

I will list out the major learnings.

This is the industry which requires your physical presence, especially when the scale is small. There must be physical presence and constant monitoring. There two way to achieve this, described with all other learnings below.

1. Location
    Having the right location of restaurant is more important than the look and feel of shop.
    Just because you found the shop which is having an elegant, or a fantastic elevation with a lot of buffer area, and higher visibility doesn't mean you will get customer walk-ins.
    You can choose even a smaller shop, but the locality or the place restaurant is very important. It must be a place where repeat customers or the first-time walk-ins should be high. New customers will not have any prejudice of your menu. It is solely based on immediate requirement to answer hunger and thirst. Best locations are near bus stands, schools, colleges, offices. Malls are good too if you have the budget for it, that is.

2. Menu

    The menu is based on the locality, you cannot decide menu based on your favourite dishes. Even the number items on menu are decided by location and your scale. Understand the location, define your scale, menu will appear.

    Different cuisines have different needs, do not try anything which falls under the category or "good to have". In our case having a Tandoor wasn't an option at all. There was clear disconnect in understanding and the price was paid.

Basically, even if you are having enough budget for a mid-size restaurant, and the location you could get allows you only to have small restaurant, just follow the rules of the scale. This will keep you in profit for sure.

3. Size or the scale:
   There are 3 scale of restaurants:
   I.   Small sized
        One cuisine - Limited number of items + optionally just-1 item from a second cuisine. Cook, helper, cleaners – Self-service styled restaurant. 1 - Cashier + Supervisor – could be just you (full time)
   II. Mid-sized
        Three or more cuisines – Comprehensive list of 1 cuisine, limited items from 2nd and 3rd cuisines.
        Cooks, assistants for each cuisine. Helpers, waiters, and cleaners. Supervisors and cashiers.
   III. Large sized
        Three of more full cuisines - Fine dining. Increased number of waiters and Supervisors even at the dining area.

4. Setting up the infra
   Locality and scale, decides cuisines and menu, including the number of menu items.
   These in turn decide the equipment and furnishing.
   Last but not the least, the sourcing of equipment, know which one to buy refurbished, and which to

have new. Depending on the scale there is lot of scope to optimize the initial capital & thereby increasing the chances of success.

This was learnt the hard way, when we had to dispose the equipment and furnishing, came to know about the whole market around this, out there.

5. People management

Number of people you employ is strictly based on the scale. You cannot afford to make either the menu bigger or number of people. It must be according to scale. Only optimization of operations and quality needs to be done.

6. Marketing

Have a budget and plan for marketing every 3 months or so. Use this rotationally on different kinds of marketing.

7. Sales

You must expand the service beyond the physical presence, as much as feasible, while keeping the profitability. Now, there are lot of options with food ordering apps and delivery. At that time there were no online food delivery service.

8. Operations and Technology integration

The number of hours restaurant is open, the timings of operation, and the shifts arrangement for workers, must be based on scale and menu. Use technology as much as possible for monitoring, billing, accounting, vendor management, etc. to reduce the working capital and increased efficiency in operations.

9. Innovation

    There must be constant innovation in all the areas to increase revenue and profitability. Use Kaizen methods in the areas which has maximum room for improvement. Mainly focus on:

    a. Menu.
    b. Expansion.
    c. Customer attraction and retention.

With all the time, money and energy spent we got a great lot of learning, which could be clearly used to establish a small or mid-size restaurant. Looking at the experience above you can see that, trying out anything or starting out any business, will require experience or the right research.

There are details to all the points discussed above, such as the negotiations done with various vendors, the agent, party catering orders done, home deliveries tried, lunch contracts done to offices nearby, etc. Description of all that requires a book of its own. The real-life case study presented above, and the high-level summary is very good starting point for setting up a restaurant.

Broker with 7 sites - Story

Now we will look at another real-life first-hand story, where I met a broker with seven sites. This is very interesting one. This happened little time after I had started my career, having completed university education and having been able to secure job as a software engineer. Initially worked in a few start-ups, this was the time of dotcom burst. After a few years got into bigger multinational companies operating. After around three years, with a total experience of around five years I was getting in to the corporate mumbo-jumbo, especially getting involved with "save the taxes", "invest in mutual funds", etc.

This is kind of the first thing that happens, buy a site or a home, to capitalize so-called low interest rates, save the taxes on the interest paid, create an asset, high appreciation value. So, this is where I began too. As you can imagine in a nine to five job, you will only be able to do all research and activity in the weekends. With the limited time, and the weekdays, especially in the earlier days of the career you will not be able to or not be interested in going out of your workplace, due to the high enthusiasm to work more. Basically, this kind of interest in the job is the reason in its first place you landed a job in an MNC.

There is an industry around this of real-estate who have either flats or plots at considerable distances and high projected appreciation, just for you. They are not really trying to trap in terms of negative sense, but they are trying to get the market, maximize their profits by targeting the people who are supposed to or who are most likely to buy.

They provide free service, in terms of visiting the site, doorstep loan processing, government office work fluff reduction. They will come to your office or your home pick you up and drop back. This along with all the news articles and projects collected such as, five kilometres from here a new highway is coming up, two kilometres from here a software campus or factory coming up. This road main road is going to be expanded to 200 feet road or 150 feet, metro line nearby just few kilometres from here, etc. All this, along with tax saving deadline, makes a very convincing story to buy.

Now that you have already decided to buy this from the perspective of saving taxes and you also see that there's going to be a high appreciation in, say 10 years. You don't really try any idea of searching further or thinking of any other alternative investments the only the question is which one of those agents is going to convince you faster. It is during this process I met a broker (real estate agent). He is the one who takes people to visit various site locations. Talking to him while going to the various visits, I found that this guy owned seven sites already, basically he had bought them on his own. Ok, now you should understand clearly this is not the I am going to buy, or any corporate worker is going to buy, using a loan to paid back in 10 or 20 years. He already has seven sites on his own name, no bank is going to give an agent any loan because he's not part of any corporate and cannot show any high salary and promise his future time to the bank. Now, do you call that a limitation or advantage? He has bought all those with hard cash.

How's that possible, it's very simple if you look at the price in the markets. Around at that time it was about 1000 rupees per square feet. Commission is 2% for these agents, now that these are off city limits, they sometimes get 4% commission. Now, just some simple math will clearly tell you how he built his own asset. Every weekend, that is two days around 20 people for the visits. Each of the property has around 100 to 150 plots or sites on an average.

These agents are associated with multiple properties at any given time. So, each weekend around 40 potential customers, visiting at least four or five projects he has in his hand. With 52 weekends there are at least 2080 customer visits. Now add the public holidays which are around 15 – 20 which doesn't fall on a weekend, 2000 visits are easy. There is a conversion rate of at least 10%, as these are not just interested people visiting, but the ones who are spending time to visit the projects, also they are visiting multiple of them. Now, with around a minimum of 20,000/- per site/flat sold he clearly has (10% of 2000) each giving 20k, easily he can buy 4 sites/plots in a year. He had been working as an agent for more than 5 years. If you look at the number now, it sounds like just 7 sites! Looks to be a small number for him. Here you could easily add all his living expenses and commute costs.

Trying to get the overview of what's happening here, he is a person who has not spent 16 years in his formal education or cleared interviews and having worked all throughout the weekdays, and midnights. He is busy only during weekends, because not many will ever come and visit during their workweek, unless it is registration of the property bought, which is taken care by the property developer, even if it happens it will all be within five o'clock in the evening.

All this is around 10 years ago, now we can imagine how many more he would be owning and the appreciation of the 7 he is owning for a decade now. At least 4 of them would have doubled for sure. He already has asset of two crore rupees ($250,000) easily. Without the full formal education of 14-16 years and the hassles of excelling and getting through a corporate job and there after working every month he has built a comfortable life. Of course, not every broker or agent might have reached where this guy goes to, because of their habits, etc., that would apply to any other profession too.

At that time, I didn't really get to these numbers and analyse the way I have done now. It was very different. At that time, I thought, I was doing much better! Just out of college got a job and few years into it I'm talking in lakhs, didn't realize that is a loan, not really what I owned right then. I would feel like a king (kind or customer is king treatment being given, not much I realized, there were 2000 to 3000 of them he meets every year!) in front of the broker. But, if you look at it closely, he's the rich person. I am able to talk in lakhs, he's owning them. Basically, I have promised my future time of 10-15 years to the bank. He owns this future time.

You must be careful about what you're really getting into, so here comes the concept of assets and liabilities. Assets are the ones which put money into your pocket. Liabilities are the ones which take money out of your pocket. This is one of the most important concepts I learned from a very good book "Rich Dad Poor Dad".

Salaried friend Story

My salaried friend Mahajan's smooth transition to financial freedom!

I will now talk about another story where you will clearly see that how, if you do some right things, even unknowingly, at the right time, you will be in an amazing state by having earned a lot of money and be able to do whatever you want to do in life. But that happens to a very few people, and the rest must make sure, they consciously get to it. I was lucky enough to meet one of them, who somehow did it right. This happened when I had worked for around 10 years (5 years after the broker experience). At this time, I wanted to add some more academic value to my career, so went on to get another degree, and enrolled for part time master's degree. This is a very straightforward step any technical professional or any software engineer would take.

It was during this time I met the person called Mahajan, who was also working in an IT company. He also is in the same master' degree course, and he was around five years senior to me. He had bought and sold many of the flats, by then. When he started in the industry there and consequently buying flats, he realized that the appreciation of flats went very high by the time construction was complete. It was right in the boom time, where people used to book flats, even before it was fully constructed, basically when foundation was being laid the booking would be done for the entire project. Within 6 months or 1 year, the price would have doubled. It appreciated greatly because there was a lot of demand and supply had not yet caught up.

The person who paid initial margin and the loan availed could be transferred to the next buyer. This is what he did multiple times and was already and had tripled his margin amount, by then. He started with around 10 lakhs and he had tripled it. At the time when I had met him, he planned to accumulate around 50-60 lakhs shortly. Five years after I met him, I see that he has launched his own company. Basically, he too used the same system, of corporate job and trying to save taxes, but doing it 5 years earlier mand focussing just on flats, not the plot and house, he built a huge capital, and launched on his own.

Comparing this to myself, who had bought sometime down the line, and getting into building a house, which didn't really give such an opportunity. The case of Mahajan my friend happens to 20% or 10% of all the people whoever buys real estate. Not everyone will be able to make this kind of an attempt or leverage and be able to accumulate the capital.

At the same time when I bought there was another person who bought a site in a different location. I bought in the northern part of city and he bought in the eastern part. The one in eastern part has appreciated four times over. He could save a lot of money in commute and everything. This shows, even if you are doing the same kind of investment, getting the time and place right or at least one of them, results could be lot different.

Just because you attempted or did the same thing, doesn't mean you will succeed. You should know exactly what you're trying to do for success.

2. Vacation planning

How I decide the length of my vacation?

Now, how do I decide the length of my vacation or the number of days in my vacation. People in a nine to five job or in small business decide the length of vacation by first looking at the whole calendar checkout the festivals or government and company holidays which fall around the weekend. Now there are a lot of circulations that happen on the web and in the companies saying things like: "If you take one day off you will get three", "If take three days you will get five", etc. Looking at the festivals which are not really celebrated at home or the government holidays which fall near the weekend and try to club them along with their leaves to make sure they have a very good number of days available. This is not really a great way, basically:

You are trying see when You are free?

Have you written down your time to someone or something else and needs to be granted to you back for some reason? At one level this looks like a slavery. It's not about how many days you need for the place or you need the vacation for, but it's all about the number of days that are available, or possible to avail with your leaves, and the weekends or the company holidays combined together.

The next step is looking at the places which you can accommodate in these days. So, this percolates to the places you visit also, not just the number of days you can visit!

It's not about the place you want to visit really, but you will just shortlist the places which can be done in those many days. The only other option, if you have sternly decided on the place to visit, the number of days are fixed by compulsion not choice.

Now, you will look at any deliverables near those dates, such as any releases that can happen or any new programs that are coming up, any sales targets, year-end or month-end or quarter-end coming up, if any of that happens, then it's a drop saying it is not possible on that weekend. Sometimes it is booked so much in advance that you might thinking everybody is going to ask at the same time, so you do this immediately and get that from your boss. It's too far off so you get the approval with the caveat of, "You can take it, but you know right, if some critical thing comes up, how things work around here". Anyway, you apply happily and book the tickets and seats and make sure that you get at them at best price possible, and hope no critical thing comes up at that time.

As the date of vacation nears you start getting worried about or thinking about every task and event if it's going to get in the way of your vacation. Will it be fine? What would I tell the family, if in case have to cancel it? So, the length depends on chances of weekend and the number of company holidays around it, your leaves available and above all the permission from your boss, and last but not the least, project deliverables. In the worst case, an issue might really pop up and you have to change the date or allow the family to go on and you'll will try to catch up in half through if possible. not be able to join saying that you will join later, or it can also happen that you are in between the vacation and you have to reduce the number of days and get back to office. Either you come back on your own or you bring the whole family back from the vacation, many of the times it only because someone thinks it is a very critical task and you have to handle it. It might not be really a critical activity, but only because someone said so.

One other very obvious thing every 9-5 worker or small business owner misses to observe are the ticket rates and crowd for the for small vacations (over weekends) such as, amusement parks, theatres, buffets, are priced higher on weekends and lower on weekdays. Again, there is no sadistic set of people deciding this, but it just the way it works. So, a person working all weekdays tries to visit anywhere pays up more, compare it to an affluent person, who has most of his weekdays also free, is able to get the same thing for lesser price. The icing on the cake is, he will also enjoy lesser crowd everywhere!

If you look at the people who really plan and go for the vacation during the usual holiday season, you will see the crowd and cost works against you, basically it works the nine to five people. You can clearly see this in amusement parks where queues at each of the ride will be huge, so you not only pay high price but also have to waste your time, and while getting back to home, guess what you face the extraordinary weekend traffic, just from the amusement park even though it is on the outskirts of the city.

It's not that someone is conspiring against the 9-5 workers or small business owners, just that it is way it works. If you see these people form the majority who pay all the taxes, follow all rules, make companies grow, so obviously these are the ones who have to pay high price on vacations too?

Solution is not that everyone should get out of this model totally, it has its own benefits to some extent. Certainly, you should not bear all the brunt of it, just make sure you build your Money, Skills, and Income sources in such a way, that you can enjoy the simple benefits which in turn enhances your performance and happiness drastically.

This whole arrangement of the society with all the formal academic and employee structure is a result of requirements from the Industrial Revolution, which happened centuries ago. It is designed to make sure people are fed properly and are getting sheltered properly, because at that time, there were only simple machines. These machines needed a lot of manual effort to produce a lot of items such as food, clothing, shelter, and the equipment required for them. This was the main purpose of the education system, to get workforce. There were no limits on how much to work and produce the goods, so everyone worked a lot. This reached its tipping point and there came May Day, regularizing working hours of a day to 8. That was beginning of formal vacation building into people's life. Now, with the advent of newer and newer machines, vacations should have naturally increased to a large extent, since most of the work is done by machines.

Still, it hasn't happened as the need and comfort level of people also has gone up.

This is the first time ever some thought on wellbeing of workers began. Otherwise, the trend was to get the thing done by workers as long as they can do it. Right from the Kings' era during which big things like the Wall of China or the pyramids or the big temples, etc. were built only by using simple machines and lot of human labour. People were used like slaves, either formally declared so or not, but the concept was the same. The same thing continues in its basic form even today, though there are lot of small fixes along the way.

With the advent of all the huge machines, artificially intelligent systems, on an average people should have had more time compared to any time in history. But the surprising thing is, this is the era where people don't even have time to spend with their very immediate family. In olden days people used to spend time with extended family and even community. What should really happen is that economics should focus on higher level of comfort, exploration of human mind capabilities. Though this is happening, it is in a very limited manner, with very few people. Money should rotate around the conveniences rather than the basic needs. Instead, the disparity has increased between the classes of people.

Though the innovations in technology and what is being done and could be done with it has reached a different level with unbelievable level of automation, dramatic communication capabilities across the Globe, Artificial Intelligence, etc., people are working even more, with lot less vacations, all this is just due to the lack of understanding on how to use technology. Not many realise that you don't have to be an Engineer to make technology serve you, and the other main issue is importing of dreams from others voraciously, without any thought.

Everyday stand guard at the door of you mind.

-Jim Rohn

The whole of economics is changing from its roots. There is no reference in history to the level of change happening right in the foundations of social-economical-political status of human beings. If you don't see this, and use this to your advantage, you would have missed the greatest opportunity ever presented to a human being.

When do I go out on vacation?

We have already seen earlier, how people including myself, being part of the nine to five cadre, really decide the number of days in a vacation. Basically, do you really go to the vacation or the place where you want to go at the right time. It might not be the case as all your vacations are usually based on the availability of holidays, your leaves, weekends, and the coincidences of the project deliverables, market demand or business demand, or the urgency of other things, at the time of vacation. Rather than thinking of what or when a place needs to be visited. This especially happens whenever you are trying to plan and visit a place for exotic places. Some might be able to do such kind of vacation, or travel to such places in the right time, only once in a lifetime or twice in a lifetime. For that they plan for three years, accumulate money for long time then get on with, and maybe they are not even enjoying the place peacefully when they are really there.

Usually what 80% of the people do is try to make sure the timing of the visit is conducive to the plan rather than what needs to be done. So, it's not about the place of vacation, and the time, when it is the best time to visit, but only in terms of possibility or feasibility, when the project permits, or the market demand permits. So, this directly ends up in two major problems which you will see, or might really ignore saying it is part of the game, which is compromised quality and quantity of vacations.

The crowd you face when you're trying to visit the place in the wrong season might be different, the hospitality, and all other things will be totally different when you visit the place in the wrong time.

A very few set of people who are big business owners, or the owner or the smart business, or smart workers, who really know where to work hard, and when to work hard, and how to do that, are able to utilize the opportunities that are made available by rest of the society, which is 80%. So, they will go on the weekdays to the places where it needs to be visited with the less crowded with the less pricing and also enjoy the comfort and also enjoy the travel commute to the place with because they choose time according to what is the best way to do it not, whenever it is available or possible. All this can happen only if you remember those people who are living out of their Thriving Abundant Money (TAM), and not those people who are living out of the Immediate of Surviving money.

Make sure you get to a place in your life where You not only decide, time, or length of vacation, but also the timing of vacation, based on what needs to be done, rather than what is possible to be done because of the compulsions you have built up.

`

How much do I budget for my vacation?

Now we will see how people usually budget for any vacation. To start off, a list of things to done will be made. It starts with the number of people traveling. Next will be travel costs, that is the commute method to and from, either by train, bus, car or whatever it is. The third is the staying cost that is the hotel accommodation, Next is cost of food per day, how many days you're going to stay there for all the people, and some buffer added to include the snacks and other things that you will be having in the place of vacation. You will go to the places of interest in the local area of where you are visiting, the cost of fuel if you have your own vehicle or you'll be deciding the amount of money for local commute. Next will be the entertainment cost or the one which you will spend for things like the purchases of tickets to shows, monuments, amusement parks and various other things. You will budget for the purchases of souvenirs. Once all these things are put together, total accrued cost is looked at.

If the budget is high, you really think what to do about it. The first thing you will try to change is the change the mode of travel, then the number of days, then try and reduce the number of purchases. So, the first mode is trying to attack the or reduce the quality of travel, by going from economy to multiple hops, or changing the time of travel to odd hours and or change your whole mode to train or bus, or whatever it is. The next is you will try to change the or manage or reduce the quality of stay, saying that it's not really required this much of expensive resorts, so we'll just get back on the smaller ones or the more expensive more inexpensive ones and things like that. The next thing you might try is to reduce the number of days. This keeps on happening until you get the whole vacation under your budget. It's not about what is required for that place or how much is required for this vacation, but it only depends on the amount of money you can spend or afford.

Now, some people might say, "No, I never compromise on the quality of vacation for cost, but I will reduce the number them, if required (take 2 instead of 4 in a year)". If you look at this approach also, it is still coming from a person operating totally from ISM not the TAM.

You should carefully have a look at yourself and introspect and realize the right way to budget your vacation, not from a point of concern but only from the point of view of what is worth of the place, and the number of things that can be done there. Remember, the time you spend will not come back again and you will not be able to go to the same place again just to do the same thing. Just think about it, if you're not able to spend a good amount of quality time and money comfortably the first time, how would you expect it to be done the next time. Unless you plan up and work on TAM, your expenses will only grow. So, you just do not have another chance at it no matter what. This is one of the common things which people usually face which needs to be changed, best part is it can be easily changed. There are lot of people who have already done it and already living that kind of life, who already have been able to generate income from more than one source. This is what we should focus on and be able to enjoy the vacation for what it is worth.

Life style Comparison Story

Now we'll look at an example from my own experience, where I was working for a Government scientific organization, which is equivalent to federal government in the US. This is a scientific research organization where a lot of scientists' work. This is not a typical Government organization where people get paid for just having the job. Here real work happens. The workforce here mainly has people with a doctorate degree. This means they have spent more than 25 years of academic study and are consistently good in what they have been studying and doing. They have been able to prove that they are innovative and on top of the things. This is about one person who I met Dr Radha Krishnan, who had been working for more than 30 years. He was almost at the near the retirement age. What I could really see of him was the kind of restrictions, he was working under. Basically, one day he had to go out for our two hours on his personal work, for which had to take permission by submitting a written small slip, kind of a, letter to his boss, and get the approval.

It was a huge campus, and you are not allowed to bring your vehicles there, so we had to walk out the whole place to get out of the campus, so it would take such a long time to walk out the gate, get your personal work attended to and return back, with swipe in time recorded. Imagine the kind of restrictions he is really working on, in spite of having a doctorate degree and having worked for 25 to 30 years in the same organization.

He was in the process of constructing a house for himself at that time. Maybe he was around five years from retirement at this point in time, now finally being able to get a plot and construct a home of his own. This is a scientist in one of the top scientific and research organizations, having spent all the time in a nine to five career. Other thing was about the mobile phone usage in the campus. No one in the campus could have a mobile phone at that time, it was in around 2005. Imagine scientists were working in such a restricted atmosphere where you in the mobile phone was not allowed. This was a huge restriction.

Compare this with a businessman who would have started around the same time without having to do, so much of education, would have really started a few years earlier. Maybe he saw some failures in education and even in the ventures done. Usually around 12 to 15 years of education and then onto his business, where he didn't really have to be so much controlled and restricted. Now this person after 10 years would be able to his own house and be able to live and do everything whatever he or she wanted to do, that too on their own terms. They use the latest and greatest gadgets, greatest now electronic gadgets such as mobiles, and be able to go around attending any personal work or newer ventures, whatever! This contrasts with what happened to Dr. Radha krishnan piling up all the educational qualifications by spending most of his prime time working in a restricted environment. Of course, there are benefits to it, but in the long run it just loses out.

Also, he or she would have taken vacations comfortable, whenever he wanted to, without having to take permission from. He's able to use the same gadget for his personal work and for improving his business. If you look at it, he is able to build a house in just 10 years, the one which he wants, and wherever he wants it. Add another 20 years to it you can imagine, at that point he would be enjoying a lot of time absolutely living on his own terms.

Restricted Vacation Story

Now to my own experience. I planned a vacation with multiple places to visit along with my family and I started on the same during the holiday season. This was all planned well ahead of time, around the six months ahead of time and having jotted down all the plan and created a clear plan of which place to visit it and where to go from where and everything, and all the places visited and all the places listed down, and also the sphere the travel mode, and the staying places everything decided and booked off in most of the places where you could really get a booking. It all worked fine until the time of the vacation arrived, just around three days earlier to the vacation we got into critical situation in project where some planned deliverables were not happening on time. Some issues were found during the last phase of testing and we had to really step back and put a lot of hours into it.

Not only me, many people had to change their plans but mine was a little more aggressive and elaborate but so what I did was I really didn't want the whole family to be caught up in this one. Cancelling the whole trip because of me didn't sound good, and I really hoped that we could get it resolved in a day or two more. Kind of work for 12 to 14 hours a day would get this done, in fact we as a team could accomplish that within two days and fixed it. I had cancelled my travel ticket alone, in railways, you could just cancel one ticket from list, and have the rest retain the reservation. I planned to book a bus so to catch up with the family wherever they were when the work was done. Of course, I couldn't visit all the initial places, but that was still fine, not having to miss the whole vacation, right? I had made a clear itinerary and given it to the family so that it's clear where they will be and when.

Once the issue got resolved in two days, I was able to start on the trip. Though it had an initial hiccup it started work. This was fantastic, I was really happy that I was able to make it, reached the place and then we just continued the vacation. Now after around three days into vacation again I get a call from the office now this time they say there's one more issue now, this an external issue which has come up and requires immediate attention, and it would be great if I am in office. So now at that point I was really very excited about the activities I do in office. So, I jumped on getting back the task, this was the time when work is more exciting than vacation. This is not very uncommon, it is usually this kind of excitation on the kind of work being done, which in its first place gets most people get into the corporate job. Informed the family that I'll be going back, and they can continue, and return once done. This was kind of a shock to family members, and with some convincing, they were fine with it.

I cancelled my ticket again, this time the return ticket of mine. I just booked the ticket back, there were some hiccups, where I had to call up some colleagues get the booking done, as it was a remote place and internet at that time, was not so great in all parts of the country. Now, when I was experiencing this whole thing, I was not really shocked, or worried about a thing. I was just thinking it's fine and it's a normal thing that happens for anybody. And I could really do the same kind of trip again but, as anybody can guess it's not so easy to repeat the whole vacation. Irrespective of what happened at the time when I look at it retrospectively, I just think, "Was it really a good thing which had happened, or could it have been better?"

One aspect was good, that I was all excited and happy about the whole thing, even though an observer would say, "That was really bad, he had a bad vacation". But, somehow for me, I had enjoyed both the vacation and resolving all the issues that came up. Though, not sure if the same kind of thing happens again, the response would be similar. The main point is you cannot be in this state all the time, it can happen once or twice, but if this is always the case of most of the time then definitely something is wrong.

It is better to disassociate your physical presence with your income as much as possible. One time occurrence is not the problem but repeat of this, definitely is. Something on the line of saying, "Fool me once shame on you, fool me twice shame on me". Getting into such a situation and responding to it, out of choice should be the case not responding to it, due to compulsion.

Euro trip - my observation

Now another story of a colleague who went on a Europe trip with spouse. Both of them were working on a corporate job. They had planned one year ahead of time and built-up savings using schemes involving mutual funds and various other things to budget and prepare for the Euro trip.

This is required very much when someone is travelling to a place of high currency rate. There's also a lot of things to be researched such as, transitions, places of visit, travel agent discussions, etc.

As far as people could see they really did take a good vacation. It was of three weeks and once they came back, they shared some experiences of their vacation out there in Europe. The whole of their planning and the budget was decided on various factors. The conversion rate, obviously lot of planning is required to absorb their own resistance in terms of, do we really need to spend so much on the commute, each of the meals, etc. Though, no one can know the exact details of all the plans and the budget, but it should have been based on the earlier discussion we had on budgeting of vacation of anyone living ot ISM. Everything such as, food, the stay, travel mode, the local commute, etc. With all the done and having done the trip, they are back and seemed happy. Looking at it closely after having talked to them for some time and getting description of the complete trip, whole picture of what they really enjoyed became clear. It seemed that they were really enjoying around 60 to 70% of the time but 30% of the time we are really worried, and not so happy about what really happened. For instance, one of the necessities, a small inevitable thought of cost of each meal is converted from pound and euro to local currency. Mentions of a pound for every rest room usage nagging sometimes. Anyone can imagine they would have been in such kind of restricted mode, at least 50% of their trip due to budget constraints the vacation is not full-fledged recreation and rejuvenation as it could have been, despite after spending so much.

From the 9-5 job or small business owner mindset this looks acceptable, kind of it will be this way, and is there is no way your budget can far exceed or be able to comfortably accommodate whatever we want to do. But if we look at it carefully, it is really possible. It's not that you're asking for super luxury that you're living in some very 5 stars, etc., but at least for the small things you should not be worried. The budget should definitely be doubled if not 5 times, of what covers the basic vacation budget. It's not really so difficult, just doubling your income every month, would easily get this done. Now, how it that possible? You have to acquire a high paying skill or leverage whatever skill you have and double the income to generate the budget required, rather than restrict the vacation and the comfort, according to the budget. Many people just realizing the potential of technology are able to increase their income multi-fold. You could spot a couple of them easily, if you just look around carefully. Some might have done consciously, others just by their coincidence such as, the company of people they keep, or the state of mind they usually have due their paradigm, or just that the timing worked for them right. Remember, my friend Mahajan's story or the broker with 7 sites, discussed earlier?

Basically, you should use some of your free time to generate the right kind of income, and contribute to TAM, and use it. Best leverage is to make money from money, and from technology, only then you'll be able to sponsor yourself and your family comfortably. It is not quick or easy, but definitely worth it, over the long time and pays many times over!

"If you don't find a way to make money while you sleep, you will work until you die."

- Warren Buffett

It is very important to understand and leverage technology, business process, and above all "higher need for human comforts" of our age to achieve it. Was it no possible in olden days? Of course, it was possible, people used to have banks giving out interests, private lending to people, renting out real-estate, equipment, etc. We can clearly see many examples of even Kings getting loans from the business communities of their kingdom, of course I am referring to the ethical Kings who walked this Earth. Just try to imagine even in those times, there were some people who used to make money out of money! That just baffles me. I got this concept after years of working!

It would be really something beyond ridiculous to ignore this, especially in this era with so many machines and intelligence built into them. Not just that it is available, there are so many people around having done it too. It will be a lot to miss out in spite of so many of them even telling how they did it. I don't think there is any excuse for not doing it and be able to enjoy the vacation as it should be.

3. Why are vacations needed?

Necessity of vacation

Now we will see, what is the requirement for having a vacation? and does everyone really require a vacation, what kinds of vacations are there. To start with, we'll just look at an analogy, one of the exciting things we would have watched is the F-1 car races. You would have been fascinated and captivated on those races, at least in the childhood. The way they go around in laps, the way they take lead, take turns, apply breaks, the sound of the acceleration, crashes, and last but not least the tire changes.

After a fixed number of laps, you see the car stops at the pit stop and people just rush in all around the car and replace all of the tires, re-fuel, replenish the oils, check the parameters and get away, allowing it to continue the superfast race again.

Now if you observe that they have just changed the tires which were brand new to start with and there they are, within two or three laps changed again. They are done! They are just done!

Now compare it to the normal car which people use for commuting or for normal usage of a family or office. These go on for a very long time compared to F-1 race cars, or any other race cars, very clearly. Usually these need to be replaced after 10,000 km or might be a few years. So, compared to the number of laps, it has lasted many times over.

This is hundreds of time longer life in comparison. This could be directly compared to the way people use their bodies. The most important thing is you just get one, so make sure you use it the right way, the way you want it.

People might be cheering and excited to watch you go on a race,

OR

They might be amazed by the way you have been using it for years.

Either way you will get people who will be amazed. So, choose the kind of audience.

Don't design your life based on audience, design your life and choose your audience.

-Srinivas B T (yes, that's me:)

Basically, you (internal audience) should be the judge and no one else. To start with it might not be so easily possible, so begin with the right external audience, then shift to the ultimate internal one! Decide for yourself, "Is it only about reaching the destination as soon as possible?" Or "Is it about reaching the destination and having some picnics along the way?". It's entirely up to you.

You could do few short sprints when on highway or a freeway, still using it as commute and travel car and still be able to last a hundred or thousand times more than a race car.

In India, around 2007 there was a famous CEO, the youngest at the time, of one of the big multinational companies. He used to do all kinds of super achiever things at the same time.

First of all, he became CEO of a world-renowned multinational company at a very young age. He used to work out heavily in the Gym. He used to run marathons. He used to sleep for four hours every day, and that was he pride too! Everyone was amazed how he could do all that in such a short span of time. To top it all he never looked stressed out from outside. One day he died after his Gym work out due to a massive heart attack.

This shocked everyone in the corporate world and outside of it. All the image people had built and the inspiration and motivation it had generated was shattered. This forced many to think on what could have caused it. It's obvious that he used his body like a race car. It's fine, if that is what he wanted to, but most of the people might not really want to do that. Whether you consciously keep account of it or not, the body will. Especially, when there is no rest given or any opportunity to rejuvenate.

He might have done even more amazing, no one could have even neared his records easily, if he had taken a break and furthered again. The most important thing you should understand is the difference between causing an injury to your body and strengthening it. Basically, there is a small difference, or thin line between these two activities. For the general public observing from outside or for ourselves also, if we are not so intelligent enough, both will look the same.

There is a point wherever you would have stretched your body to the maximum capacity or very near to that. Now, you could allow it to rest and giving it the right kind of nutrition. Body and Mind both have their nutritional and time (rest) requirements met. Once given these three, the Stretch, the Nutrition, the Rest. Magic happens! It builds itself to the next level.   It's not going to replace just the tire you wore out. It will upgrade everything. Remember it's not replacing with an equivalent part, it will better it every time, if you allow, that is!

On the other hand, if you just go a little further and a little more, just that this time you are not providing the required nutrition and time for it to rejuvenate, you will just damage it permanently. It will not be evident directly on the first day or the second or even the first year, but it will happen. So, if you keep on doing it for the number of days, of course it's all worn out.

In the same analogy, what happens if you continue to run on the F-1 car without having replaced the tires. It will burn out and rims will touch the road and start burning, very soon there will be nothing left to continue the race, what race? You will not go anywhere. So, the only question is, how do you plan to use your car? It's entirely up to You!

Now, to fully clear the real-life example we used, compare the CEO with Arnold!

Why are vacations needed?

Arnold used to work 5-6 hours every day in the Gym. Then, he went on to become Mr. Olympia and Mr. World. He definitely knew how to build the body and keep taking it to the next level. Did he stop there? No!

He went to acting classes, and accent removal classes to improve his English to overcome his childhood and his home-grown German influence. He went on to become a super hit world class hero. Did is stop there No!

He worked on his social skills and contribution the country he immigrated to. Learnt the necessary skills and talent required to enter politics in the immigrated country. As if that is not enough, he went on to become a Governor, which is the highest political position any non-American born citizen could get! Now imagine! I mean, remember! For this is a fact! He achieved world class things in so many different areas, one after the other. He became a legend! I don't mean to say, he fully finished one thing and then only got on to the other. He clearly worked on multiple things at a time, still knew which one to be on the highest focus at any particular point in time.

Clearly, he has given due consideration to the feedback from his own body and mind. He has worked with his Mind and Body to make sure he builds upon and makes it resilient, ultimately doing an incredible journey in all the areas of life.

If you get too greedy, and try all of them at one shot, you might end up missing the finish line in any of them! You cannot afford to be ignorant. Ignorance is not an excuse; you have to make sure you are keeping track. So, use your car carefully, for this is a magical one! Either you can multiply it's life and capability or divide it, and you don't get a replacement! Decide, it's all up to You!

You have to be careful in identifying the point of no return, and never touch it. Always return before the point of no return. The beauty and wonder of Mind and Body is that if you keep nearing and the point of no return, get back, rejuvenate and try again you will see the point-of-no-return has moved ahead. So, you can stretch a little more. A little more next time around, that is how you multiply your resources! So, remember not to touch the point of no return, but return before that, even much before that is fine. You can clearly see the earlier difficult stages are very easy now. This is an easy way to cumulatively build on your strengths.

This you will be able to easily relate to swimming. First day when I went to learn swimming it was really exciting, splashing water all around with a tube and enjoying! 2-3 days into it, there is no tube and I had to hold the railing and move the legs. Then, comes the time to leave the railing, immediately I am going in, drink water, everything is messed. Oh! Man! What is happening here I was thinking. Then 1-2 days later it is still the same! Now I talk to my fellow students, looks like I am not going to learn swimming (feeling almost certain of it). Yet after few more days, I could do a very short distance, like 2 feet. At that point it's really amazing, now came the hope it is possible and few days later, I can clearly swim. Now came the next challenge, swimming across the breadth of the swimming pool. This seemed so tough, every time I start, I have to get back to the same shore. Sure enough, one fine day I am done with the breadth of the pool. Then, the same thing with length of the pool. It's basically same in everything we try, just make sure you don't get killed by hard work, you will excel like crazy!

Pains of vacation

We will have a look at how usually people decide the length of their vacations. Basically, why do we require a vacation? We will look at that first.

Vacation is basically required to make sure your mind stays really active, and consequently it gets your body also active and healthy. What usually happens is *"All work and no play makes Jack a dull boy"*. This only not only makes your mind dull but also the health of your body deteriorate.

If you really rejuvenate at least annually or once in between a long haul of work, you will really be able to perform better, and your health will improve drastically. There are many therapeutic methods, which recommend just a vacation in the right way, kind of silent retreats to recover from even serious illnesses, especially some the chronic diseases. Vacations not only answers the mind's requirement to stay focused on whatever you work, but also body to be very active. A common observation which most of would've had is being able to solve some issue, which has troubled for some time by just giving it a break, not thinking about the problem for some time. Just looking at the problem from different aspect or angle.

No problem can be solved from the same level of consciousness that created it.

-Albert Einstein.

Basically, changing the state of mind to higher level of clarity and awareness, by thinking of some totally different, inspiring, or peaceful thing we get a new perspective. This is also a vacation at one level. Your mind jumps on newer and newer things in different environment it automatically rejuvenates itself and when it comes back, it looks at the issue in a whole new way.

Many of the solutions to big problems have come out people when they were not really working on or thinking of the problem consciously, but when the problem was on the backburner or enjoying something else and conscious mind was totally free. This is in fact the subconscious mind at work, it was working on the problem which conscious mind was trying to solve. Magically it can solve many problems. Many scientists have openly admitted that their greatest invention or discovery were found in their dreams.

Now there is a new trend or technique of lucid dreaming, it was used in some ancient cultures, Tibetan or Buddhist, which is being able to control or being able to consciously dream whatever you want. Basically, not right from the beginning of sleep, but once you are in a dream state and just before the sleep totally breaks, there are techniques to consciously drive or divert to the place where you want it to be. It's not so easy and so often you could get this, but whenever it happens it is a surreal experience. Many affluent people who are also world class performers use these kinds of techniques to visualize and create their self-image and easily hand over the problems to sub-conscious mind. All this requires kind of time and state of mind, which the busy 9-5 workers or small business owners don't usually get. Of course, the world class performers are also very busy, in fact much busier than the former, but there is a key difference. The key difference is whether, you are busy by compulsion or you are busy by choice?

Are you busy by compulsion or by choice?

– Srinivas B T

To start off, you should be taking vacations to be able to really understand what the contribution really is, it can do wonders even for your regular job and problems you face. Your vacations could be celebration with family or friends, could be going out and meeting a friend after a long time, or visiting some exotic place. Sometimes even looking at the pictures or videos from a previous vacation puts you in a very high state of vibration, a high state of happiness, satisfaction, and peace. Many of us would have certainly experienced even if it was a long time back or for a small time, Now, think of people who really take a really nice vacations for a really long time, obviously their performance and energy levels, problem solving acumen will be great.

You will also be able to learn newer better and faster, that easily translates into your bank account big-time! Now, guess what, you have more money to do more vacations, what a positive cycle to be on? If you have carefully observed Life is always a set of cycles, you should make sure you are always on the good, positive, inspiring ones. Somehow, over a period of time, especially if you are not conscious of it, you will find the positive cycle you were on has slowly turned the other way. Don't fret over it, just change the cycle. It might be easier sometimes and little tougher sometimes, but surely anyone could change over, starting with small changes if huge immediate change is not feasible. Sometimes just the awareness of you being on a negative cycle, puts you back on positive one. There is a very subtle but super powerful lesson here.

If you carefully observe the mind (your mind) doesn't really care whether you are on positive cycle or on a negative cycle. It enjoys depression as much as blissfulness. It is You who are suffering and the people around you who are suffering when you are on a negative cycle. So, unless You decide and take action, mind once in a state, will keep looking out for more and more reasons to make it bigger whatever it is.

Here comes the other aspect of mind, which you can and should use to your advantage "doubt", in any of the positive or negative cycle, there comes small flashes of doubt on the current state, use it to jump out of negative cycles, and watch out and ignore or get more clarity by studying, when "doubt" appears during positive cycles.

So, getting onto a positive life cycle and staying there should be your aim always, and one of the easiest ways is to take vacations.

Types of vacation

In fact, you can observe that, however you use the body, it will just give the results accordingly. There is no magic to it, except for the fact that it will be able to generate a rejuvenate and get stronger, if you allow it to. The other thing, if you have observed, is that there are many marathon runners at the age of more than 90, just google you will find them. A lot of people who were marathon runners, even at the age of 90 they have been running along the way, maybe it's not as fast now, but they have lived to tell the tale. So, it's all up to you to decide whether you want to use your body as a race car, or the one which sustains and travels the whole wide world lives to tell the tale.

Now we will look at the kind of vacations that will be required. Small thing, such as a weekend is itself a very big thing. This is the time which you could really use to rejuvenate for a week. Usually, it is just one day that you will be rejuvenating and other day it might be for shopping, or some self-pruning, just grooming your hair, double the shower time, lazing around, allowing your mind to wander around, etc.

If you take some monthly two or three days off along with the weekend making it four, it will really help in keeping yourself fresh for much longer. Similar thing happens when you take a yearly break, like some companies have a furlough, allowing people to take around a fortnight of vacation. That is really rejuvenating and motivating. The euphoria kicks in before the vacation and stays for some time after the vacation. You will be in a great mood to work and your efficiency will naturally go there is no need for you to artificially induce any motivation or get motivated. The need for self-discipline to kick in also gets delayed. Just the thought of the vacation is nearing by and your plans and your idea of living in a vacation itself will bring you such an enthusiasm, and spirit that we'll be able to do all things efficiently, if you have observed that carefully. The small caveat here is about the furlough of company giving you the vacation, so there is no risk of a project task sabotaging the vacation, otherwise it could be a whole lot different experience, which we have discussed earlier.

So, irrespective of company having a furlough or not, you should be capable of taking such a vacation.

After the rejuvenation you will clearly see it takes a good number of days to really come down, before that if you are able to activate it and keep it alive by taking the one or two days of a small vacation, you will be able to extend the inspired working state greatly. It's not that it's impossible or not by not being done by anyone, just that very few believe or realize it' possible. In any work culture or organization there are the percentages people either way, captured by the "Pareto's Principle" of 80:20, who achieve this.

Not everyone is able to, because it requires a lot of care and focus in what you do, and also a lot of self-discipline, to keep your spirits high all the time. That means you have kept the mind in control, more precisely befriend your mind and make sure it works for you 80% of the time and not against you. Definitely not everyone is aware of it, and the majority of people get into some or the other trap, either externally induced or internally created by their own thought and emotional limitations.

There are so many thoughts floating around from others, which are really packaged well to be incepted in your mind, especially in this era of information bombardment. Many of the times you will not be able even distinguish an advertisement from information, it is so blurred, there is only a thin line between separating them. And very few recognize. Simple examples would be binge watching some videos or reading a blog, which are totally meaningless to what you want in life or enjoy doing, just because they made it look attractive, you are watching it. There was a thumbnail or some initial attention capture by dopamine triggering techniques, your emotions get invoked and then the captivation happens. This is all fine, if that is in your area of interest or what you really enjoy, but many are caught unawares, and hours and hours are gone by.

There are lot of algorithms, the super advanced ones, having incredible kind of data to predict what you would do next, so that platform is active on your device and your mind as much as possible. So, the more you stay on the platform, the more ads they can show you and the more they can sell to you. Not maybe immediately but definitely at some point in time,

You have to make sure that you are in control and understand and see when you're deviating from what you plan to do and be able to achieve.

Nature's built-in vacations.

If you look at it carefully vacations are really built into everyday activity of each and every person, organism. Now, let's look at the everyday cycle of sleep, this is a vacation for your body and your mind, and it has to be met, irrespective of who you are, how much of achievements you have done, or what kind of levels, your body is at or your mind.

Very rarely some people have been able to skip for a few days, but definitely you will have to go through that cycle every time, so basically the sleep is a vacation for your mind and body every day. So, the same thing gets extended to various levels like at a higher scale like weekly, monthly, yearly. This has been basically designed for human beings to be able to perform their physical activity to produce goods or to provide services for people in a very efficient manner so that they live longer and be able to serve and be able to prosper along with being able to provide the service or the producing the goods, which they do.

Now, before the advent of the modern era there were many kings who got a lot of work done with giving any proper vacation to people. If not all, most of the huge monuments were build reducing people's life spans. Even long after the dictatorial kings, there was no clear vacation of work hours defined until May-Day resolution, fixing the number of work hours.

Not just for humans, there are cycles even for seemingly inanimate things. For instance, the daily cycle of Earth rotation, no vacation just heat on one face of the globe, would have it burning. It's just so much built into the system. The yearly cycle of earth going around the sun with a full season of Heat and dryness, which moves fine sand carrying a lot of nutrition and minerals from the deserts of Africa to the Amazon forests, across ocean.

Could you imagine, that Sahara Desert helps the Amazon forests by providing the nutrients when, all the nutrients and various kinds of minerals, get dried up, and it's blown across the ocean into the pores of Amazon, which really use them to enrich their own forests. Forests helps the desert rains from across oceans. Basically, everything is a cycle, just one kind of activity will surely destroy whatever it is on to all the time. Everything has to take a vacation, the dryness, the rain, the cold.

Why are vacations needed?

Human beings can use the conscious mind along with their subconscious mind and whole lot of help from the natural cycles. You're able to design your own vacations, fortnightly or quarterly or half yearly or whenever you require, based on the work what you do. Whatever stress you build upon a particular part of the body or mind, or particular emotion exercised all the time, you should take a vacation according to that.

Just the everyday built-in vacation, which is sleep and dream of every person can be used to create magic, not small, but really magical appearing innovation and solutions to problems. Some of the greatest inventions on the planet, from the top scientists have been during their dreams. There are many scientists, some for the greatest, who have admitted on this, without worrying whatsoever on the lines of, "Scientist talking of dreams?!".

So, it is not all about the conscious mind capabilities, which have indeed created amazing ideas and converted them into reality. Still, when the subconscious mind takes up a problem, it's a different ball game altogether. Many scientists working on a problem for many days in a row couldn't find a solution and somehow were able to push it to the level where subconscious mind takes interest in it. Once that happens, magically one day, one night, in one dream, they get the solution.

Benzene

Did you know that structure of benzene was discovered by August Kekule in the late 18th century, after a dream of snakes? Can you believe that! He was struggling with the atomic structure of benzene, but he could not really get it solved, understand how these molecules can be connected to each other with the bonding requirements of each element. He was unable to find the solution to this problem and one of the nights in 1865, as mentioned by him, he just dozed off trying to solve this and in his dream the atoms dancing gradually arranged themselves in the shape of a snake, then the snake turned around and bit its own tail. The image of the snake, with its tail in its mouth. It continued to dance in front of his eyes, and then he realized, it needs to be a ring.

After he woke up, he could arrange the carbon atoms, using the same form seen in his dream, satisfying all the chemical bonding requirements. It was unbelievable, the structure was first of its kind ever proposed until then. Before that point it used to be only a chain of molecular structure that were discovered, this gave a whole new direction, and everyone was really amazed at this happening during a dream. If you see, it is a vacation for the conscious mind and subconscious mind was engaged, voila you have a fantastic discovery. For centuries, it was one of the most innovative solutions found. After that many things have been happening, but those are only incremental, but the first one is kind of beyond human capabilities.

Theory of Relativity

Next is the greatest discovery of current world, the theory of relativity. Can you imagine the possibility of relativity being found by Einstein, not while thinking and trying to solve the problem, but during dream? He had done the major part of the solution or the maximum that his conscious mind could do, but the ultimate solution came from the dream. What happened was, as it is recorded, he was dreaming of walking through a farm where he saw some cows, and they were all jumping across an electric fence. He saw all of them jumped at the same time, and they all received electric shock. At the same time a farmer who had been standing on the other side of the field saw them jump one after the other, like a Mexican wave.

Voila! he realized now that the same event happened was different for different people, based on where you're standing. So, if you're standing, from standing point of view, what you see is different. This is literally unbelievable, years and years of work, trying to understand and theorize such basic but, seemingly beyond human capable, laws of nature revealed during dream. Once again, a major discovery during, what you can clearly call a vacation of conscious mind, and the sub-conscious mind returning from vacation for brief time!

The Periodic table

Now elements on the periodic table. This revelation of a pattern of elements, kind of a breakthrough came during a dream. Mendeleev was trying to find the right way to organise the chemical elements. It had been on his mind for months together. One fine day when in 1869 he wrote the names of elements on cards. Used one card for each element then wrote the properties of each element on its card. He could see, somehow the atomic weights were important, but could not really figure out a way or any meaningful pattern.

He was feeling that he was close to uncovering the mystery and discover something important. He played around with the cards moving them for hours straight and slept off doing that. Hours later he woke up and found that his subconscious mind had the magic for him, with a logical arrangement of elements.

Now mathematics!

Many people, including the top mathematicians of the world at that time, were baffled by the theories and conjectures written and some proven by Srinivasa Ramanujan. If you look at his achievements in the field of mathematics, it's just mind blowing. Even with his short lifetime he created around four thousand proofs, conjectures, identities, and equations all in pure mathematics. The notes he had written kept the top mathematicians of the world busy trying to understand, for many years after he was gone. It was basically futuristic mathematics, he used to come up with, which had no match. He noted down theories. One of the top mathematicians of Cambridge University, Godfrey Hardy, who had worked with him expressed that, if mathematicians were rated on a basis of pure talent from zero to hundred, and he would rate himself at 25, Littlewood at 30, David Hilbert will be at 80, and Romanism a perfect 100.

This is one of the top examples, can you imagine getting a perfect 100 from the top mathematicians of the world at that time for a person who came from no formal education, very little formal mathematical education came up with top class pure mathematics, which were beyond the times. Ramanujan clearly said:

> *"While asleep I had an unusual experience. There was a red screen formed by flowing blood as it were. I was observing it. Suddenly a hand began to write on the screen. I became all attention. That hand wrote a number of results in elliptic integrals. They stuck to my mind. As soon as I woke up, I committed them to writing..."*

Why are vacations needed?

Imagine he's saying that he directly got everything, not just some visual thing and he converted that into an equation, direct written equation appearing in the dream. Not that everyone can sleep and get such extremely magical dream but, definitely you can solve the problems you are working on, for sure.

Law of natural selection

Even if you see the law of natural selection by Alfred Russel Wallace, he got it during his dream. He had been asking the question of how new species could arise, but could not ever find an answer, but in 1858 he had an extreme dream and hallucinations caused by a tropical fever. When the fever went away, he found that the theory of evolution by natural selection had come to him directly and he just jotted it down. If you observe, what is happening here, whenever you get involved, with your subconscious mind you can solve a lot of problems. It's amazing the way in which structural analysis, logical analysis, mathematical analysis, works out, there are lot of problems solved. Now, if you look at any problem which is at the end human knowledge, then nothing logical is going to get the solution. Here comes the subconscious mind to rescue.

The subconscious mind is the one which takes care of all the habitual behaviour or humans, and almost all the activities of human are habitual. More than 90% of whatever anyone does is dictated by the subconscious mind. All the decisions made, routine activities carried out, right from brushing with your prominent hand to deciding or using the route to you take to office, shop or gym, to the life changing decisions, are from the subconscious mind. Conscious mind basically deals with all the sensory inputs. It also uses the various mental faculties, such as imagination, intuition, perception, etc. to solve and problem you face or to enjoy the life you have. It helps you to interact with everybody and everything around you. It is like a jet plane, what you make out of it depends on how you use it. This in turn depends your learning of its capabilities and how much you learn on using it.

The defence and the sleep mechanism are handled by the reticular articulating system of the brain. This helps to put the mind and body to sleep state, though it means lot different for body than for mind. On sleep mind gets into another set of activities, it doesn't really reduce and stop any of the activities. Body on the other hand stops responding to basic sensory inputs, though they are active and still capturing all the inputs, most of them are ignored. The body gets into a repair mode also, during the sleep, where it rejuvenates and reconstitutes all the injured tissues. Though this also happens during the waking state, it is of much lesser scope and scale. The point here is not to discuss the total mechanism of repair and rejuvenation during sleep, but to clearly establish the importance of sleep which is in fact a vacation designed and built in by nature. We have seen the clear examples of people who get carried away by trying to impress others, ignoring the basics and pay the price. Also, examples of people who have peacefully and efficiently used the mechanism to come up with legendary solutions.

The other important distinction that needs to be made is about the mind and the brain. Though brain is a very important and huge constituent of individual's mind, it is still a part of it. The mind is much more engulfing and projected out, it is really hard to clearly identify the borders of it. This is not my discovery, it is mentioned and acknowledged by so many world class scientists and philosophers for centuries now. It is currently known that an average person faces around 60,000 germs every day. The numbers might vary depending on the living conditions of each person, but it is around that huge number. All of them are taken care of, in terms of detection and handling these automatically. Producing the right kind of antigens, antibodies, attacking and clearing them off. All these are functions of brain and neural system co-ordinating with various organs including the endocrine system happens without any intervention of conscious mind and thought involved. These are influenced by the state of the conscious mind, but not really known or understood by it. This is not clearly understood even by the latest medical research. Basically, you don't have to know how any of your internal organs' function, just maintain the proper state of mind and the physical activity, rest will be taken care of.

The details

The point of all this discussion and bringing out the inconceivably great capabilities of brain, and body is to understand that:

You cannot and need not know details of how it all works.

A very similar thing happens with technology and the use of it. For instance, the details of how all the avionics systems, such as electronics, software, communication technologies, need not be known to learn how to fly a plane. You must learn just how to use them, not try know how it works internally.

To get properly rejuvenated and perform at almost at superhuman level take the right number of vacations and give the required intervals between each of them. Also get the comfort level of each vacation proper, so that, it really helps out rather than adding to the frustrations of financial and time limitations.

You can look out and will be able to find many people who have done unbelievable things in terms of innovativeness and the quantity of work. All this is possible with the kind of automation and business and service process available. Many of these activities in the olden day had to be done by the person himself or herself or delegate if feasible.

The machinery and the automation available now are playing a major role in alleviating the hardest physical labour and risk of injury from human beings. Though not as extensively as it could be done but wherever possible.

There are a lot of people who have been using such, latest and greatest technology to free themselves from doing the routine work, which any machine can do much in a much better way. Whatever you're doing, check how to automate, if automation has not reached to your domain of work, either you change the domain of your work, or try and get a skill which uses automation to earn an extra income. Even if you are not making money out of the time gained by automation, you can give a vacation to your body taking it to a higher level of performance, and you can live the human life which you are born to be.

You should not be living like a machine doing the work that any machine can do either now or ten years from now. It will really look ridiculous, when you look back and see that you spent your whole human life doing something which a machine could do much better, a lot faster, with quality, and in higher quantity. Make sure that you're on the right cycle and try to achieve time freedom, at least by using the techniques of who have already done it. Even better would be to invent your own ways to achieve it, so that people are amazed by the way you did it and better theirs!

4. How to earn meaningful money?

Evolution of professions & businesses

There are various innovative ways in which people are earning money in the 21st century. We will briefly look at the history of earning money and how it has evolved through the ages, so that anything we look at could be analysed in terms of how far it can go. There are various transformations that have happened throughout the history of mankind. Basically, there are three categories of earnings, which services a particular type of human need:

1. Primary
2. Secondary
3. Tertiary

Primary professions are the ones which are answer the basic needs of humans, such as food, clothing, and shelter.

Secondary professions take care of basic comforts such as, commute, travel, basic education, and medical care.

Tertiary professions go from basic comforts to luxury, the entertainment industry, higher education and research, excursions, etc. These are not the necessities of human beings but is a good to have.

All these have evolved to a great extent from the time along with the human evolution. The first set of things are just to use the very simple machines to simplify the purpose of agriculture to produce the food, and to be able to provide the basic needs of food, clothing and shelter. With the Industrial revolution, lot of advanced machines were invented, along with electricity. These started doing a lot more things which could not be done by human beings at that scale. This kind of revolutionized production in various sectors such as agriculture, clothing, shelter. Along the way it replaced a lot of traditional jobs fewer people required to operate the machines. This naturally came with the new requirement for learning the operation of machines and also to invent newer ones.

This directly had an impact on the education system where people were needed to learn operate and service machines, invent and improve them. So, education system started producing people who could these activities and produce a lot of products answering either primary, secondary, or even tertiary needs of people. Next major shift was with newer and improved transportation, using oil, which enabled commerce in a big way. People started realising that a lot more things can be done by replacing muscle power by machines, which created a new set of them.

Next came advances in telecommunications with innovations in the semiconductor industry, and commerce went global. Advanced machines with automation using embedded computers started sophisticated manufacturing started with CNC (Computer Numerical Control) machines. This became the new normal where it was not just replacing the muscle power of human beings but foray into muscle skills. At this time, it was not just multiplying the number of products it was about replacing the human muscle skill. This is stage two, of advances in machines. A lot of people who were thinking that this cannot be done machines had to move on to the next level of skills or settle with lot less compensation for their work.

Third stage of advancement is when machines started addressing human physical conveniences. It is not just an incremental change to the existing machines, but the fundamental way in which machines operated as machines could now remember things and adapt to the newer inputs presented to them. It is not just the routine work or skilful work of a person, but of a team, as the machines were capable of responding differently to different inputs changing the whole job market. These were only seen in sci-fi movies earlier, which was a major disruption to traditional companies, and many established professions, operating over decades or even over a century.

The newer companies based totally on the newer technologies, just within five to ten years of starting up became much bigger than almost half a century or a century old companies in order of magnitude bigger. It was not just technology led companies that were disrupting the existing norms and accelerating the evolution, but also the application of technology in various fields, such as e-commerce. Physical brick and mortar shops started getting replaced, and many of the people who did not adapt to the newer technologies went bankrupt. Some of the initial challenges requiring human experience, not just specifications and feature descriptions, to buy such as, clothing was overcome.

Professions, jobs and businesses evolved, and newer ones were created while thousands were totally replaced, rendering some of them are totally meaningless. As we already saw companies like Kodak went bankrupt, because it did not adapt and only gave the opportunity to some other people who invented the same digital technology and brought it to market.

Kodak is almost gone now whereas it, could have continued to be a market leader, if it had adopted the new technology and moved on. Just trying to extend its life by not showing the new technology doesn't help, as someone or some company will find the next innovative thing. There is no option for you not to adopt it is only a matter of time. Whoever moves first and fast will survive and thrive.

Now we will look at the evolution of robots. Robots started right from the beginning of the industrial revolution.   In the simplest definition Robots are machines which can do work replicating human movements. These were basically used to manufacture. Though it started in that way, with the advances in semiconductor, software industries, the original use of robots has changed drastically.

There is a level of intelligence built into the machine, starting just with eight-bit controllers, and the first moon rover, the one which could walk on the moon, and collect some data, along with camera. The first robots could respond to the standard inputs and giving standard output. It would not adapt to any newer inputs. All this was with 8 or 16-bit controllers with limited memory, and as the semiconductor advanced robots also changed drastically. Now robots have been even assisting in medical field to the extent of performing surgery, especially the minimal invasive ones.

Robots can do a lot of work, which humans cannot do, such as surveillance, checking a mine field, surveying the weather. This is the second stage of development in robots where they could replace the standard thinking process of humans. This was clearly demonstrated when it could play chess with a human being. To begin with, it was done by feeding the computer with an algorithm. Basically, algorithm a defined set of steps to convert a specific kind of inputs to a specific kind of output.

Initially, what would happen is it will learn a set of steps for playing chess, and use the memory built into the computer of all the previous games, so that the machine could predict all possible move of the opposite player (human being), and then respond. If you look at it, mind power was getting replaced by the machine. As we saw machines started with replacing muscle power, then then the basic muscle skills, and now the mind power.

The weather systems or a supercomputer is fed with all data whatever is available and has been known. The measure of various parameters and how it resulted in a weather pattern, is fed into the machine and it analyses all of them and tries to predict it based on history. This based on the huge memory, and predict based on closest match.

Next level with the evolution of artificial intelligence and machine learning machines can now learn from the input data also, not just using the built-in algorithm. It is kind of a dynamic algorithm which changes based on inputs and over time. It uses feedback and can change the way it responds to the same set of data at a different point in time. Just like human beings they learn and improve their response over time.

This is the biggest ever disruption that has happened and is continuing innovation furthering it incrementally, every passing day. There was a movie "Terminator" which frightened people and many criticising, saying machines could take over and eliminate human life on earth. It was too early to say, at that time, after around 20 years of the movie something on those lines are really happening.

In very recent times, there was an experiment conducted by Facebook with AI, in which the machines started talking to each other in a language not created by any programmers or of the human decipherable one. The machines basically started talking to each other, by creating a language of their own, supposedly using AI. Power had to be pulled out of the machine to get them stop what they were doing. This shows, what AI can go up to. After having admitted initially that the machines were talking in a new invented language, which drew lot of criticism, it was clarified that the robots never invented any language, the machines were only trying to simplify the conversation and derived a shorthand communication.

Elon Musk usually expresses his concern on AI that, he has said that artificial intelligence will be vastly smarter than humans and would overtake the human race by 2025. But that doesn't mean that everything goes to hell in five years. It just means that things get unstable or weird.

The other interesting this is, to know what is happening with the Sophia kind of robots, one of the humanoids. It is called as humanoid as it looks like a human being and also that human thoughts and emotions are getting built into these kinds of robots.

The humanoid (robot) Sophia from the Hong Kong company Hanson Sophia looks like it has almost reached AGI (Artificial General Intelligence), though technically it has been concluded to be an advanced chatbot with AI, with facial and emotion detection capabilities of human beings, it can see. Though this gives a visual idea of Robot for many, there are so many robots, which normally no one recognises.

Many of the robots could only be visualized as software robots, as they operate on distributed hardware. Also, they might be majorly operating remotely on some server sitting in some data centre. They would only be collecting data or using the data sent from mobile phone, laptops, home PCs, or even the CCTV cameras and other sensors connected over internet.

Some of them have grown so big by accumulating data from millions and millions of people and storing them in huge data servers, and using processing servers to mine meaningful data, that they are bigger and more powerful than governments in some countries. It might not be far that, some of the companies who have built such robots and own them could have a great influence on policy making for citizens.

Congratulations!!!

You have done a great job of completing the first important part of this book. This is the one which answers the "Why" part of it. Using the most popular strategy of setting a SMART goal, which will make sure you will achieve it. We know what this stands for:

S : Specific

M : Measurable

A : Achievable

R : Reasoned

T : Time bound

Reference from Wikipedia – below:

Hysterical strength is a display of extreme strength by humans, beyond what is believed to be normal, usually occurring when people are in life-and-death situations. The classic anecdotal example is of parents lifting vehicles to rescue their trapped children. The extra strength is commonly attributed to increased adrenaline production, though supporting evidence is scarce, and inconclusive when available. Research into the phenomenon is difficult, though it may be possible as adrenaline is known to affect muscle twitch and endurance.

In 2013, in Salvage, Newfoundland and Labrador, Cecil Stuckless, a 72-year-old man lifted a Jeep to save his son-in-law pinned underneath

In 2015, in St. John's, Newfoundland, Nick Williams lifted a four-wheel-drive vehicle to save a young boy pinned beneath its tire.

Reference from Wikipedia – till here:

How it is possible? It is only because the **"Why"** was strong, very strong.

Not all of the examples, illustrations, real life stories might have directly resonated with you, but you would have understood the perspective, co-relating to similar experiences of yours. This will make sure, all the limitations that could come to you such as, "I don't know technology", "I am too busy", "I am old", "I am too young", "I've tried many, none worked till now", will vanish. If you have built a very strong desire, rest you will get done, for sure.

The next important thing you have shown is, patience and persistence, many give up after a few pages of reading, for some reason or the other like, "This doesn't apply to me", "I know all this", "I'm too busy". Patience and persistence are a very important virtue, you should possess, though you might be working fast to complete things, there will be a waiting period, just like gestation for seeds. Once set out the Robots will start working for you, gradually depending on how much you are interacting with it give what it requires, it will keep increasing its work for you.

How to earn meaningful money?

Now that you waited for knowing what are Genies, and how to make them work for yourself, I will describe in the rest of the book, the biggest and most popular one out there.

These are very dynamic ones and keep changing with time. So, once you have gone through the examples, check them out practically for yourself. It might take some effort to get it started, once it's done, you will know how to get the next one.

Mega Machines and Robots!

Are You using Facebook, YouTube, Amazon?

Or

They are using You?

Now we look at how robots are involved in human life, more importantly how deeply? We have looked at some examples of robots, but if you have observed the soft robots are much more powerful than the physical ones which you can see like Sophia or the other machines (rovers), which are walking the moon. These soft robots are the ones which use human emotions and human resource itself as the input. These are the ones like Facebook, which basically has all kinds of human emotions and celebrations stored and locked up in their database. They wish you on your birthdays without fail, and are even able to predict, how you might be feeling and adapt accordingly.

They help you celebrate, even better they remind your friends and family to wish you. They understand you and your desires much more deeply than anyone else could, as they know everything what you searched, liked, disliked, followed, wished, and spent time on. Not just that, they also have the complete information of which product you would like and the service which could help you out, along with what new is coming, and find analyse if you would be interested in it. All your activity like the posts, comments, searches are analysed using AI and machine learning.

As you can these soft robots are much more powerful and resourceful than any human is, as they track each and every activity including your physical movement using GPS on your mobile device. All of these are integrated together and analysed. This is reason Facebook, Google, Amazon, WhatsApp, YouTube, Instagram, etc. are such fantastic and wonderful tools that ever existed in the history of mankind. It has data of more than a billion people, no human being on this earth, nothing else can match the level and scale of these soft robots.

Google.

This one kind of revolutionizes the way people think, interact, and people find things. This has all kinds of data of what people search. Whoever has any presence on the internet like sent some emails, searched online, read blogs, watched videos, listened to podcasts, something which has been consumed online will be on the database. Billions of people on the planet have done all these or some of them at least. These are analysed by Google and able to find each and everything which is relevant to you. The data which you want exactly, it learns from the way the user clicks through to reach any website and how much time spent on website and where he or she goes from there. All this is stored along with demographics, which is the age of the person, gender, nationality. languages spoken, etc.

When you search something, after that find out whether you really bought something or you just did research and didn't conclude anything, and if you went back, say after two days or three days it has everything tracked and analysed. With this it presents to you, based on that you can present a different set of data or much more optimized. I have also seen from my own personal experience the price for some products change based on whether you buy first time or later. It uses your data not only to optimise your experience and help you conclude the purchase, but also includes it in demographics so that same kind of product and services could be presented people in similar situation as yours, and interest.

Maps

Google maps obviously knows your current location and every person who has used it, also it knows your home, office, etc. Even if you are Apple phone and have used Google Map anytime it's the same case.

This is used for traffic prediction and the way people are traveling on road, this does a kind of super traffic policeman kind of job. It has so much data and that too live data it can optimize the routes for every person, just imagine that power for a moment. I'm not talking about 1 person or a 100 or a 1000. It can do this for millions of people all across the whole wide world, in their local time and location, using processing power, memory, tele communication network, internet, satellite network for GPS, and that on your local hand-held device of laptop. This is not possible by any human or traffic police however smart agile and good they are. All this within a matter of seconds it recalculates and suggests various routes with estimated time and exact distance on each.

Even after having really understood what these kinds of robots are doing, and if I am still thinking that I require some more help to better my life, it will be the biggest opportunity ever lost.

If you have checked the monthly report of movements from google maps, it knows each of the place visited, how long you stayed, whether it was overnight, what mode of commute used, etc. This is used for the betterment of services to the person himself or herself and also be able to predict the behaviour of others and the various businesses around.

YouTube

This has a different kind of capability, of course most of these being free platforms to start with and work the way people come in and respond to each other is just mind boggling. The robots on YouTube of course, learns all that and keeps presenting to you the next thing, with such an intelligence, that you will keep watching the videos. There are some Ads which are relevant to you and be able to direct to you to the set of things which you are looking for are and were not able to conclude earlier. These are relevant to your local place and according to the demographics. This understands and keeps learning with every passing second and interaction of people and presents to you the right kind products and services to enjoy, educate.   There are a lot more such things available, we are just discussing the top ones and the biggest ones to get the complete picture of capabilities these have and the ones they give us.

Amazon

Amazon is one of the biggest search engines, which has the people who with their credit card information, that is people with capability to buy. This is the biggest platform with such a qualification.   The majority of people who are searching on Amazon are not searching for just research purposes or entertainment, but seriously looking to buy ready with their money. Just that their needs and requirements have to be met, they will buy. This amazing robot which actually optimizes the kind of products it shows to you is more financially powerful first-hand.

Of course, it uses all the kinds of resources and capabilities we have discussed earlier and sells products that you can consume and educate yourself with. Amazon basically started as an online platform to sell books. There are hundreds and thousands of them added to start with, then moved into other products, which now is the world's largest B2C and C2C eCommerce platform.

Earlier it was very difficult to publish books and a lot of great ideas were not getting published. This was revolutionized by Amazon by bringing self-publishing to everyone, basically it bought out a company called CreateSpace, which is now part of KDP (Kindle Desktop Publishing). This gives opportunity to anyone who wants to publish. Now there are lot more of them such as Smashwords, Kobo, Notion Press, etc. Many of these now provide tools and offer help so that you could indie publish your book instead totally self-publishing, which will give professional quality to the book and also avoid all the incredible delays and issues of traditional publishing.

LinkedIn

This one has data of professional people working all over the planet. There are CEOs, directors, engineers, doctors, sales and marketing professional, advocates, pilots, you name the profession, and you will find here, including students who are currently studying. Though it seems not much on the direct sales front at the first look, there are lot of businesses built on and around this platform. The robots working to keep this platform on top and expanding, of course does most of the things we have discussed till now.

This has also caused a lot of disruption in the traditional job search companies and HR (Human Resource) departments, from small start-ups to huge corporations. Many companies like Monster have been majorly replaced by the search on LinkedIn. It LinkedIn also has provided capabilities such as being able to recommend a person, see their career progress, which could be very easily verified, without having to employ specialized services for that. Checking out the professional history and the work experience, the whole concept of getting references have totally changed. Professionals and students can now look for and get connections to a huge network which greatly helps in understanding the latest and greatest happenings in their domain of work, enabling them to drive their career, very efficiently.

The other great benefit is anyone can do a proper research and understand other domain of work or profession, than their current one, without having to rely on any consultants' capabilities, which come with their own prejudices and biases. These have helped millions of people to make money to not only survive but also thrive in this new marketplace.

IBM's Watson

The next one we look at, is IBM's supercomputer which has medical data of people, called the Watson health. Super computers are first ones which had lot of processing power and capabilities built-in to be capable of run artificial intelligence software. Now the semiconductor industry has advanced so much that processors and memory are lot more powerful and smaller. Also, with advances in distributed computing, where the processing is done on many computers and result is combined to get the full solution, enabling companies like Google, Facebook, Amazon, to build their own system, partially reducing the dependency on core technology producing companies.

All these use the telecommunication network and that of satellites. Governments and private companies have to use them to achieve anything meaningful. Many of the features and software are not really available for normal people or businesses, but only for those who have created it and the authorities and governments for law and order is maintenance, surveillance and security.

Twitter

There are some big and widely used networking platform over the internet such as the microblogging site twitter, which are basically a platform. Though there isn't any big robot on these which could help normal people, it has in its own way changed journalism. Earlier some of the reports and articles would be very misleading, which could affect a whole community of people or a state, with the wrong context or by twisting the news a little bit.

Now with this global tool available to mainly the influencers and political fraternity, they can communicate to masses without getting misinterpreted by anybody else or taken out of context. This works both ways, in this case both positive! where the influencers and politicians do not end up communicating opposite of what they really wanted to say, and people following them clearly being able track what they said in the past!

Instagram

Instagram is a platform which people use extensively to share the moments of joy and be able to enjoy with close ones even if they are physically across geographies. People can keep in touch across boundaries of countries, time and be able to share and enjoy.

WhatsApp

Though only a centralized peer-to-peer platform and not much of a robot this has revolutionized personal communication and withing a group of people. With this a person can communicate almost instantaneously using pictures, speech, and videos. Compare this even to emails which looked to be really cool earlier, is drastically different and much more accessible and useable.

WhatsApp doesn't make any money from users, but you could do it using some of the marketing companies, who provide you with referral kind of opportunity to share a product in your groups and earn.

One simplest example is: meesho.com

Zoom

The software which has taken one to many communications to the next level and has clearly demonstrated that it can replace the classroom environment, known to mankind for many centuries is extreme. This is not just replacing the classrooms and conferences, but just doing it eliminating the national and geographic borders, as if they don't exist at all!

A teacher, leader, or influencer can talk to hundreds or even thousands of people at the same time across the globe. This is clearly evident especially after the pandemic or 2019. Most of the people were not able to travel attend seminars, not even classes. Even people who were lethargic and didn't really wanted to move online had to jump on it, not for thriving but, even for surviving.

How to earn meaningful money?

Basically, how we communicate, how we buy things, discuss, entertain ourselves, educate ourselves everything has changed and is continuing to do so further.

Naturally most of the businesses have changed from door-to-door kind or marketing and sales, or cold calling using yellow pages to targeting the right kind or audience for their products and services. The broadcasting method or traditional marketing on newspapers and TVs to massed who might not even be interested or requiring any of products offered looks rudimentary.

The power and relevance of robots is increasing by the hour, though some still protest, like what was done for electricity when it was initially discovered. Many people said it is very bad for human beings and will destroy everybody, looking at it today it has really revolutionized the way people live and work and almost everything kind of depends on it now.

Make Mega Robots your Money Genies

One of the passive income streams has been earnings from royalties. This has gone overboard now to newer things such as videos and small blog posts, of course, not with exact payment models, but getting the same results, in fact much better than books. Kind of without any or very low initial investments, and almost no entry barrier.

Millennials (Born in early 1980s to late 1990s) kind of have taken this for granted and contributing to a high rate of millionaire creation recently. Not just creators of super powerful robots and software application have reached the top, but many who have just taken their talent or service or product on these platforms and robots have reached too. That is Magical!

Company having 100 years of history or more and dealing with and having control over huge physical assets such as crude oil, electricity, automobiles, have been overtaken in terms of net worth, revenue and profits by some of these newer age companies. All this has been possible by using the incredibly powerful and intelligent Robots, having access to global data, basically they have no boundaries, either physical, political or economic.

These Robots can easily be compared with mythical Genies!

Whatever data you want you can get in a matter of minutes or hours. Of course, it all depends on which of the Genies you have access to and how much you know to get it work for you. It has gone to the extent of, you being able to even talk to it and get what you need. Simplest of example, not just limited to, is Alexa.

I call these "The modern genies" of the world which are more powerful than anything you could ever think of. Best is they are all available to do at your fingertips and your command. This even the kings and Emperors didn't have. Just like the saying these are waiting, after having said, "Your wish is my command".

Identify the changes in Professions

Understand the Transformations happening in industries and professions.

Now we will look at the transformations that have happened to various professions and how you can make money, much more than what could be done traditionally.

A look at the company blockbuster, it got reduced from 60,000 employees to just one shop. Earlier when Netflix had proposed a collaboration, while Netflix was a nascent Blockbuster board of directors reviewing the proposal laughed it as Netflix was asking for $50 million. Blockbuster at that time was having monopoly on the DVD rental business. Now, Netflix is worth billions of dollars and blockbuster is in shatters. You can imagine the whole transformation that has happened and how professions and business have totally changed.

Marketing services

If you are observant enough you would have noticed Google is just marketing company, which has built excellence in online dynamic Ads. But generally, it looks like a high technology company, having built one of the best search engines. Yes, it does make and use world's best software but, technology isn't the main business, like that of IBM, Apple, Oracle, etc. It specialises in marketing and advertising to the right people at the right time.

People are moving to online heavily especially after the pandemic across the world. Whole of the commute to office has changed drastically now, as anything that can be done online is done online. Also, this has opened up the entire global market, the consequences of which are yet to be seen. Rest assured there will be changes.

Now Elon Musk is coming up with use of the satellite network to bring internet with broadband kind of speeds directly to people, without the requirement of having to lay the last length physical cables. This is going to further revolutionize online activity adding to the global workforce capability and in turn affecting the consumption it generates as of now only in big cities. This is going to be huge, You have to keep a tab on it and think how would, whatever you are doing, might change because of it.

Stock markets

The other very traditional and super powerful economic instrument is going through huge transformation, the stock market. The first change which is for some time now is the De-Mat (dematerialized) shares account. There are a lot of analysis tools now which used to be only available to people with good knowledge of mathematical and analytical skills. Now it is at the fingertips of anyone, there are free tools available on the internet doing phenomenal calculations directly on the chart, predicting and projecting including previous history or movements. You just have to give the parameters and it will give you all kinds of historical analysis and predictions.

Major analysis tools such as MACD, RSI, Bollinger bands, etc. are directly available. Just build strategies and use the tools to trade or invest. Obviously when it has gone so far, you can easily imagine that this could be done by machines. So there comes the algorithms used by super powerful machines to do the same, Trading! This is called algo-trading. Some of them are commercially available where you can set the target, stoploss, trailing stop loss percentage, etc. and the machine will to the trading for you.

The good news is, the algo-trading has not taken over 100%, there are still human beings on the market, and should be there for near term future. So, you are not totally up against super powerful machines yet. Only thing you have to understand and take care of is, your own emotions, and your own skills in understanding and predicting the performance of companies and the general market trends. The main issue is most of the retail investors lose track and get into mode of gambling. There is a thin line for the non-observant between trading and gambling in the stock market. If you are entering the stock market directly, you have to know the difference, and make sure you act up on the learning.

You could follow the principles of pure world class investors such as, Warren Buffett and many others, which is easier. You to make sure you clearly understand your risk appetite and returns requirement, customize the strategy, get it reviewed by a reliable financial advisor and then follow it to the word, then you will be able to achieve your financial goal.

Gambling Vs Trading

Check how you are feeling or why you want to do, you will know whether you are Gambling or Trading.

1. If you have no journal with reasons for each entry and exit then you are Gambling, you should know which setup gave the signal for each entry or exit, then you are Trading.

2. If you are not studying the market, and the companies, aftermarket hours you are Gambling, you should spend time learning market and the companies, then you are Trading.

3. When you win if you are praising yourself, you are Gambling, you should be learning from it and look out for the next opportunity.

4. When you lose if you are blaming anything at all you are Gambling, you should be marking this as a learning in your trading journal, remember and move on.

5. If you are playing to win always you are Gambling, you should be playing to win the war, not every battle, should be taking stop losses.

6. If you are playing to feel excited you are Gambling, you should be playing according to your strategy, then you are Trading.

7. If you are playing just for money then you are Gambling, you should be playing because of your passion and for education along with money.

8. If you are socializing after a loss then you are Gambling, you should be learning and journaling it, then you are Trading.
9. If there is no growth or learning and your game hasn't improved then you are Gambling, your game should have improved over time, then you are Trading.

10.

Trading Vs. Investing

Check the reason for buying or selling a stock, you will know whether you are investing or trading.

1. If you are buying a stock sell after 5 or 10 years at a higher price then you are Trading (lazy trader), you should be buying a stock to earn from dividends then you are investing.

2. Of course, you can be happy and book appreciated stock price, but the attitude defines investor to trader.

3. If you are buying a stock only after technical chart analysis then you are Trading, you should be analysing fundamentals of the company and judge the management, then you are investing.

4. If you are checking the charts every week or more frequently you are Trading, you should be following the company results and bookkeeping then you are Investing.

5. If you are buying, because everyone is buying a particular stock, you are Trading, it should be based on the company's product or service and its future prospect.

With technologies adapted in the market the access to various derivatives have become very easy now, these could be used to reduce risk and also improve flexibility and liquidity.

Social Media Marketing (SMM)

Marketing has changed and now lead generation is done in a variety of ways. You can filter people who will be interested in your product of service and then pitch the offer.

Most of the times we are just using the same archaic methods of learning and earning money just being a mute spectator to revolutionary things happening around, the worst part is getting used by those tools. Basically, tools or the Genies as I call them are not the ones using you, it is the intelligent person who has learnt how to use the Robots and has invoked them in the right way. He or she has shown the Genies to fill the bank accounts and deliver service or products round the clock using, you guessed it, the Genies!

If you get into these technologies due to compulsion there will be a lot of price to you will be paying, in terms of inconveniences, lost opportunities, income source and wealth.

There are people who have even taken purely physical and local businesses such as real estate on to the internet space, combining various things like consultation, legal verification, financial solutions, etc. We will not discuss on those in this book, and make sure we stick to the Robots which can work and deposit money in the account 24/7.

Powerful robots such as Facebook, Google, YouTube, Amazon could be used to attract and showcase your product and service to the relevant audience. Learn and use them as the marketing tools, because they are designed for that.   This is called the Social Media Marketing strategy.

Education

You can train people for their academics, or market-oriented skills, or hands on training for people. There are easily many gaps which needs to be addressed to enable a fresh graduate or diploma holder to be employable and productive int the industry. There are also requirements of training professionals, in a particular field wanting to change domain, pursuing an interest or due to financial reasons. Now that the boundaries are obscured, you could easily find students in you are area of expertise.

Coaching and counselling.

Life coaching is the forte of people with experience in life and even if not very interested in learning newer technologies. Their experiences in areas such as inter-personal relationships, role of money in life, self-motivation, even regrets and missed opportunities, lessons of how to avoid the pitfalls, could be of great importance to people and a good opportunity for coaching.

Now, how are these related to money Genies? Aren't they just pure traditional income sources? We will see how Genies can help here…

Example: There are many educational websites which have online courses. There are a wide variety of such courses in terms of they are conducted. Some easy examples are Udemy, Mind Valley, OnMyGoal.com, etc.

Udemy.

These manage your course 24/7 and keep on generating revenue for you all the time. Majority of course content which are repetitions of the same lesson content for each batch of students, could be created and delivered using videos. You could get on live with your students and clear the doubts and conduct evaluation when required, reducing the time of your engagement for content delivery by 80%. This is not just a concept, it is being used by many people and are earning 1000s of dollars, some of them even earning a 5-figure income. This even works for a 9-5 professional having time only in the weekends and might be a few hours on a weekday. Many people who had been working for over 20 years after having studied for 15 years or more before starting on job, have been able to quit the job after two or three years of successful trainings done using online platforms.

There are lot of sites which allow you to created content and deliver online lessons such as, Udemy.com, MindValley.com OnMyGoal.com, etc. Each of them has different way of conducting the classes and focus. You can choose the one that suits best for you.

On Udemy.com you could create a sample video lesson, upload for review. Once reviewed and accepted, you can create and upload the full set of lessons of your course. Udemy does the general marketing of the top courses available on the platform and also specific courses sometimes to attract potential students. People who land on the site checkout the courses' preview and enrol on any of them if interested. Creating the course content is entirely up to you.

On MindValley.com industry top experts get to create content and deliver using the platform. Most of these are life skills, relationships, financial literacy, etc. kind of content.

On Onmygoal.com you could approach with your idea to create course, get their help in identifying the gaps and create a course to address the same. You could also get help to design and create the content. Deliver the same using their platform. OnMyGoal does the marketing of courses to potential candidate and they could preview the course they are interested in and enrol for the same.

Make yourself a worthy Master of Genies!

Make yourself a Master, who can handle Genies

Identify your interests, limitations, and capabilities. Channel, overcome, and strengthen them.

The observation

You might have observed, how one person is happy and one is sad one person, one is rich, for having fun and frolic, the other is suffering with sickness and poverty. These two people can be from the same society, school, or even the same family, but one is on, one end of the spectrum and the other is on the other end of the spectrum. How does it all happen. Is it just fate and luck, and that too, the one which cannot be changed at all? If so, who decided it that way and how long will it be like that. If you have seen things long enough, you would have also seen, some of them transform where sad and sick person became happy and healthy, a change like a night and day. Poor person become rich and some of them were able to keep the transformation forever, until they died, and also passed it to their children building legacy. While some others who gained lost it. There have been people who would have been rich, and become poor, became rich back again.

These kinds of examples you will be able to see and find in your own society, community, company, etc. What really makes the difference? How does it all happen? Is there a definite way in which this happens, or is it all just luck and circumstances and things beyond our control?

If you observe you will see that the nature operates by laws. These laws of nature are simple and works all the time. Everything operates based on laws. Just that some people have deciphered it, and some have not. Just because you are not aware of it does not mean they will not work, or they don't exist. They work each and every time and no matter what. You will have to try and understand what those are and how they work. Many mysteries of olden days have been answered by science. Science basically is a set of experiments to ascertain a particular process or result based a particular inputs and actions performed. If there is a set of actions leading to same results consistently, you have deduced it scientifically, and it is possible to replicate the results.

If you see the laws work so precisely, as Bob Proctor says, that even you can put a man on a satellite go to space and come back to earth safely. There are thousands of satellites revolving around the Earth, all due to precise laws of nature that always work.

One interesting example from history is of Wright Brothers inventing the airplane. Everyone was sure that, it was not possible. They were saying these guys must be crazy, that they think they can fly a piece of metal, like a bird with a machine and actually put people in it. It would have been easy for many people to say it is not scientific, citing the laws of Gravity.

Now that, it is a fact where no one doubts about air travel, what changed? Does it mean that law of gravity does not exist anymore? No, it means that law of

Aerodynamics exists along with the law of gravity. Gravity works just fine, still you could use the law of aerodynamics to design a vehicle which can fly and get back to land safely due to Gravity.

Some people, if you have observed have achieved richness, after going through poverty. To understand this, we will look at the law of compensation which is one of the best laws that needs to be understood and used so that you always stay ahead of the game no matter what new technology comes or disruption happens because of political changes or conflict or for any other reason. You could thrive instead of just trying to survive.

What is law of compensation?

Law of compensation states:

"The amount of money you receive is in direct proportion to:

1. The demand for what you do,
2. Your ability to do it, and
3. The difficulty there is in replacing you."

There are three things on which the compensation depends on, first one is the demand for what you do, you should be doing something which lot of people want. If there are a lot of people who require your services or your products, obviously there is a huge scope to get clients.

The Second important thing is your ability to do it. Just because there is a lot of demand, does not mean you will be employed or be able to sell you service or product. Anyone will come to you and pay whatever is worth it, or whatever you ask for ask of it, only if it is worth it.

Third one is the difficulty there is in replacing you. If you are easily replaceable and anyone can start doing whatever you are doing, then of course, you will not be paid as much, as lot of people will jump in and competition will ensue, very shortly you will be one among the average and accordingly compensated. So, you have to take care of your ability to do it and you should make sure you are at the top or at least one of the best in whatever you are doing. If you keep sharpening your skill and honing it, you will be automatically replaceable.

Give me six hours to chop down a tree and I will spend the first four sharpening the axe."

- Abraham Lincoln

Sharpening the axe gives much better results in chopping down the tree rather than trying to chop the tree for six or eight hours. So, improving your skill is the most important thing. Now you know what needs to be done, the next most important thing is you have to know where to do it (which area or domain to apply this)?

For this identify the skills in high demand, the first part of law above. Technology can be leveraged to a great extent to multiply render service or sell products beyond your physical presence; it can reach vast number of people very quickly. This same technology is available to everyone, so the only differentiator is your skill, build it.

Identify your passion

How do you build on a skill to the best possible level? For this you have to identify your passion and work on that. Now, we will see how to identify your passion. First, make a list of things that you like to do, and write a reason for each as to why you like to do that activity and how much. Second step, is to understand which of those are:

1. Likes
2. Hobbies
3. Indulgences
4. Passion

Third step out of the activities on the passion list identify, which of those are:

1. Infatuations and
2. Desperate ones.

Infatuation based passions are the ones which you have started liking recently or, have liked for some time in the past, but could change over time.

Desperate ones, are those, which you really want to do in life, just have been able to do sometimes or yet to start on. These are the ones, which you strongly feel you should be doing before you are kicked out of this World. Yes, everyone will have to leave one day, willingly or not. Only when you bring that into picture, you will get the absolute clarity of your passion.

It's fine, if you are not able to figure out which activity makes you feel like that, right now. Just make the list of all things you like to do in life and keep adding, modifying the same often. One fine day you will get it.

Likes

Simple way to get started is to look at the list of things you want to do and find out which are your likes. These are the ones, with the little bit of pushing and prodding you can give it up, or you can change your opinion of it. I like to what this of movie or that, sometimes comedy movies, after few days or years with you started liking watching detective movies. This is just on your "like" activity. This could be also kind of things where you say, I like the pictures of mountains, forest, sea, etc. these could be changed easily or you could just trade them out for a cup of coffee, for instance.

Indulgences

Somethings like obsessive consumption of junk food, smoking, drinking, or just sleeping, or falling into depression, are indulgences. These are also the things which people who have got into feel, they can't live without it. But these are nowhere near passion and do not fall into category of, "I have to do these before I die". These are just the bad, stress handling methods that you have imported from someone. These have come from a point of compulsive action, which you seem to have no control on.

Hobbies

These could be misunderstood as passion. These are ones that you take some action on, whenever you have time. For example, you would like to have some pets, or aquarium, you like gardening in your home, cooking. Take care and taking care of your car or taking a small ride. If there is a time constraint such as some work at your office or your home you would easily delegate the hobby kind of activities to someone or just drop the idea, if haven't started it. Some people don't ever have a hobby and are very happy, satisfied in life.

Passion

These come into two categories and could be difficult to identify. Some people will have one or two others might have more on this list. These could be the ones which you have picked up from childhood and started to resonate within, whenever you say a related event, activity, or personality who demonstrates it. For instance, you might have liked the way air-force pilots, manoeuvre mid-air and walk back in formation after the flight, or the way doctors work, or artists, or automobile drivers, or philanthropists, etc. work and behave. Make your list on a clean sheet of paper. You will have to do some activity on what you write down to be able to arrive at your passion.

The list of activities which had picked up in childhood would have kept you captivated for a long time. Then, comes the points in life where you learn lot of physical realities of the world. The human life cycle, life cycle of everything around and at this time you would figure out a lot of things for yourself, with inputs from lot of people (dead or alive), environment, your own observations. You would end up in lot more questions about many of them too. After all this, now when you look at the list of passion, the real one which you are really after will pop up.

This is the one for which you will become ready to compromise any other activity. At this time in your life, depending on various factors, you might have got into commitments, which can't be just dropped. Yet, you will keep your activity on the list all the time.

This activity is not a like, or a hobby, or an indulgence.

Whenever you start doing this activity you can go on easily, working all the time without getting tired. Many times, you might have even ignored lunch of dinner doing the activity. It's not that you will be able to do it 24/7 but, will be jumping out of bed next day, when you have to work on it. You would get so immersed into it that you will lose track of time.

Remember last two requirements of the "Law of compensation". Once you have built and income source based on this, there is no limit for your happiness, as the world will pay for what you love to do. There is an important catch here. The passion you identify might not exactly match the requirement for very high demand in the marketplace. You should identify the need for your passion and address it, even if the demand is not very high. It's very unlikely that your passion is an absolutely unneeded for anyone, because anything and everything you have ever thought of, has come from whatever you have seen, heard, smelt, felt, tasted or dreamt of. Look out for it and you will find the need, it might not be in your community, state or country. It should definitely be there, find it, work on it.

Strengths and weaknesses.

Use your natural talent. For example, for some people it might be really easy to solve a math problem, for some it is writing a poetry, or understanding science, the same activity could be tough for someone else. Identify the one you are naturally good at on which other people are struggling to, develop or are average. Trying to addressing the weaknesses will at the best make you above average or good at it. You should be excellent and world class in whatever you do, so there is not option here. You have to identify and choose your natural talent and hone it. You will own it, any discussion about that particular skill and micro-niche will not be complete without mention of your name. It might not end up being some very big names like Lincoln, Mandela, Gandhi, Mother Theresa, Arnold, Bruce Lee, Steve Jobs, etc., across the globe yet it should be in your circle of influence.

Choose your natural talent and hone it. You will own it.

-Srinivas B T

Handling weaknesses

You should not try work on your weaknesses much, overcoming is not really required, in fact many times it helps to wear it as a badge. Something on the lines of Tyrion (fictional) below. There is an important catch here, please pay attention. The saying asks you, not to forget what you are, context is of the physical state of dwarfs which can't be changed, and that is not the only identity. Catch is you should also remember who you are (the strength of yours). Remember both sides of the yourself (coin), always.

"Never forget what you are. The rest of the world will not. Wear it like armour, and it can never be used to hurt you."

-Tyrion

There will be a lot time and effort required to address your weakness, and will only give average results. Remember time is the most precious thing anyone could ever possess, recognize it while you still can.

We will understand with the example of Arnold. Initially when he tried to be an actor his accent was a big hindrance, the weakness. He enrolled into acting classes and kept it going, but didn't really put all his effort there. He used work on his body building, his strength. What happened later? He got the movie Terminator, a world-class-blockbuster. The people in movie industry who had rejected him because of his accent, applauded now saying his accent made all the difference, sounded just like a machine, which was indeed the major reason for success of the movie.

Talking about Money Genies, the modern world Super Robots, no wonder I'm amazed by Arnold's achievement in Terminator.

Now the important lesson:

Arnold didn't work on, and fix the accent totally, just made sure he built a fantastic body and won accolades in that, while still auditioning for movies. Now when

How to earn meaningful money?

Terminator came, his weakness took care of itself, it just got converted into his additional strength.

This is exactly on the lines of Chanakya's (an ancient philosopher and king maker) saying:

"... names of only those will be written in golden words, who have converted their weakness into their strengths..."

-Chanakya.

It's not that he could not have remove the accent, if he had put the effort, it is very much possible and could be done. But you wouldn't have the movie Terminator, or the legendary Mr. Olympia or World. When you work on your strength and make it the best, your weakness is just ignored or sometimes gets doubled up with the strength.

The other simple way to look at it is, weaknesses make sure that you don't spend time on those activities, helping you to prioritize naturally. What would happen, if Arnold's accent was already good, and he got lot more movies, his entire passion of body building which made him a legend would have gone hidden, somewhere in a haystack.

How to render a service or create a product?

Identify if you have gained a trade skill which can be used in the marketplace to render service or build a product, which people are ready to pay for. Doesn't matter if it is formally recognized by the academia or not. There are so many opportunities, in terms of problems and gaps from basic needs to comforts of human beings, which are not addressed by formal education. There are many big corporations who also don't give much weightage to formal degrees, ex: Elon Musk's Tesla.

Formal education will make you a living; self-education will make you a fortune.

-Jim Rohn.

So, do not bother whether it is academically gained or not only botheration should be whether it is useful to people, and will they be able to pay for it.

If there is no such skill with you yet, check out the major problems people of facing and think of the talent you have naturally, which could be used to solve the problem. You have to first start by making the list of major problems, poorly or inefficiently addressed as of now. Then think of solutions using the natural talent you have assuming that you are already best in that skill. Once you have the blueprint of the product or service addressing the problem, write it down on a clean sheet of paper, don't worry the final product or service might be different. Now, go ahead and enrol in some classes or join a job, where you could hone your skill. Once done build the product or service, use technology and go global 24/7.

If you already have a job and commitments, do the same things, and build the income source, based on your skill and generate at least 50% of your day jobs income out of this.

Next best step would be to join or form a mastermind group to enhance the success. This is very important to make sure you have support system and can proceed in a very effective and faster manner. It will act as a catalyst and will also help you not do things which unnecessary, by the virtue of giving different perspectives.

Once done you will be on the highway to success.

The Money Genies

Some of the mega Machines and Robots we have seen earlier, could be purely a money generating machines or Robots for you. The fact is, many of those well-known ones and a lot more are already literally creating money for people. The only question is will you ever become one of those ingenious Masters making these phenomenal Money Genies work for you.

Here we will discuss a few of those from the money and numbers perspective.

Google

Approximate numbers of Google

1. Google's internet search global market share is more than 90%.
   So, it knows exactly what people are looking and searching for across the globe 24/7.
2. Consequently, it knows more about what people are looking for globally, then any government, or anybody could ever know.
3. There are around 2 Trillion searches every year on google.
   This is around 63 million or 6.3 crore searches every second.

4. The number of employees is more than 100,000.
5. It has a net worth of more than a Trillion dollars. Around 74 lakh crore rupees.
6. It earns more around $100 Billion annually from its advertising on the internet. That is, 7 Lakh crore rupees.
7. Gmail has more the 1.5 Billion users, that is 150 crore people. This is around 20% of the total world population.
8. There around 25 thousand devices using Android from 100s of different brands.
9. The Google's Artificial intelligence blocks around 100 million or 10 crore email spams each and every day.
10. Google maps searches every day is around 260 Billion.
11. Chrome which is Google's browser accounts for more than 60% of internet browser market share.
12. Almost 85% of mobile phones use Android which Google's mobile operating system.

This show how powerful the Mega Robot Google is, and how much influence it has over billions (100s of crores) of people, using internet. Clearly internet economy is already here and growing fast. There is no other way it is going to be. It's not just about Google, but any company will have to have internet presence in some form or the other to even survive.

Clearly there is a lot money transacted on Google. It also owns YouTube, which is the second largest search engine in the world. We will look at it separately, as that one is Mega Robot on its own. One of the simplest and straight forward revenue generating model of Google is AdSense. If you have a website, or you just have written some blogs, you could create an AdSense account and allow Google to place Ads on you site or blog post. Whenever anyone buys using the Ad, or even clicks the Ad posted on your website or blog post, you will receive a commission from Google.

So, Google's AdSense could be your simplest and first Money Genie to start with. This you could do just with your writing skill, without even owning a website. There are so many tutorials teaching this, you could just head to **www.moneygenies.com** to checkout further, on this and any other Money Genies discussed here, for an updated extension to what is discussed in this book.

This is not some new Money Genie; it has been there for 17 years now. It was launched in 2003. Of course, it has grown leaps and bounds from them. Best part is, you do not have to worry about what kind of Ads, for whom, etc. It is all taken care by Google, absolutely no thinking from you. You just have to make sure whatever blog you are writing or the website you own has your quality content. Just do whatever you are an expert on, the Ads will be based on the user profile, which is completely taken care by Google.

Make sure the articles or content you have on your blog or website attracts a lot of people, and they find value enough so that they read through and look for more of your content.

Just to put across some idea, I checked some statistics or internet and took an average of the top earners using AdSense.

The top earners using AdSense earn anywhere from $50k to $1 Million per month, that is 36 lakhs to 7 crore rupees every month!

Many internet marketing companies have come up, along way which provide alternative to Google's AdSense. Some of them are:

1. BuySellAds
2. Media.net
3. Amazon Native shopping Ads
4. Bidvertiser
5. Sovrn (Earlier known as VigLink)
6. Skimlinks
7. Monumetric
8. InfoLinks
9. PropellerAds
10. PopCash
11. ylliX
12. MadAds Media
13. Evadav
14. Adbuff
15. PopAds
16. AdClickMedia

Before starting to use any of these including AdSense, it would be good to check which works out best for your content type, the revenue and payment options they provide and the kinds of Ads they show, is there any control and management required from your side. Discussing just any one of the Money Genies, such as using AdSense, or YouTube, or Amazon, will be a book on its own. Here we will work on getting a clear picture of what these are capable of and how you could get started.

YouTube

Approximate numbers of YouTube

1. YouTube was bought by Google for around $1.5 Billion.
2. Its revenue was $15 Billion in 2019
3. It has more than 2 Billion users.
4. YouTube is the second largest search in the world.
5. It gets around 1 Billion views every day.
6. Around 500 hours of content is uploaded to YouTube every minute.
7. Its Ad revenue was around $15 Billion in 2019
8. In 2007 it launched YouTube Partner Program with Ad revenue sharing model.
9. Monetization of YouTube channel requires 4,000 hours of watch time in the last 12 months and at least 1,000 subscribers.

Top earners from on YouTube make anywhere from $2.5 Million to $12 Million, in a year in 2015. The same, in year 2020 was ranging from $15 Million to $29 million. The Robot, the viewers, the buyers, the earners, and the earnings are all going up.

This is just the direct earning model on YouTube. There are many more revenue and earning models, which many creators on YouTube use, without depending on the YouTube Partner Program. YPP requires 1000 subscribers and over 4000 hours or watch time in the past 12 months.

Some of the ways are:

1. Using Affiliate links on the channel.

2. Product reviews.
3. Sell digital products, e-books, online courses.
4. Funding from fans, even if they are less than 1000.

Facebook

Everybody knows this as the biggest social networking on earth. It has around one third of the world's population as its users. There are over 270 million (27 crore) users in India alone, which is the biggest market for Facebook. This social networking site has so many users, in spite of being banned in China, which is the highest populated country in the world.

Facebook also, like google has a very big, I mean global scale of advertising and marketing presence.

Looking at the numbers:

1. Facebook has a revenue of around $85 Billion.
2. It has an income of around $29 Billion.
3. This exceeds some of the small countries GDP.
4. The net worth of Facebook is more $111 Billion.
5. Sometime it had crossed $500 Billion.

These are just some of the numbers to show how powerful the Mega Robot is and how much influence it has with people, along with the amount money that gets transacted on Facebook. This company, no doubt is playing a major role in even shaping people's interactions and there by influencing many major decisions made across the world.

To add to all this impact, Facebook has acquired a lot of companies to make sure it stays on the top. This is the aim of every company, yet only few succeed to do this at the scale done by Facebook. Some of the major acquisitions are:

1. WhatsApp
   Messaging and voice-over-IP service
2. Instagram
   Photo and video sharing social networking
3. Oculus VR
   Virtual reality devices

Amazon

1. Amazon's revenue is around $380 Billion.
2. Its operating income is around $22 Billion.
3. Its assets are valued around $321 Billion.
4. The market cap of Amazon is well over a Trillion US Dollars.
5. This is the largest e-commerce company in the World with Business to Consumer and Consumer to Consumer.
6. Alibaba ranks first, if B2B is also considered.

Not much introduction is required of the platform and the robots it runs, as almost everyone who has bought anything or searched to buy on internet would know about Amazon. The basic numbers we had a look is just to get a perspective of how big is this compared any of the others. The number of products sold and the database of buyers and sellers it has is just mind boggling. Best part is you also could start selling on Amazon, how can this get any better.

So, this is one of the biggest Money Genies you can get to work for You!

We will look at how people are already using it:

Initial capital to start on selling on Amazon

The main issue many people face to start up a business is the entry barrier. Though this is very small compared to the other option of setting up a brick-and-mortar store. Usually, people who do not have experience of a physical shop, so there is no point of reference to compare. The cost to setting up a shop could start from $500 (Rs. 35000/-). With the kind of exposure Amazon gives for that amount, it seems miniscule. Just to get the perspective, it gets the delivery done, in its first place it has setup an online store with secure checkout out and a global brand, just these two aspects cover initial investment from you, multifold.

The fact is, around 80% of Amazon sellers have used less than $10,000 (Rs. 7 Lakh) to setup their shop. Even this amount is less than an average brick-and-mortar store having only local exposure.

Setting up costs include:

1. Sourcing [samples]
2. Fee [Amazon]
3. Marketing [of products]

It is usually better to start off with a small investment and very few or a single product. In around 6 weeks, you will be in active selling mode.

Time it takes to be profitable on Amazon

This usually varies and majorly depends on the amount of research done by the person, the time spent setting up the shop, following up and making sure the customer experience is given the right importance. Usually, from the statistics around 60% of sellers become profitable with a year of starting up on Amazon. There are some aggressive people who enter and become profitable within 3 months, though it is just 1 out 5 who start their shop. It still shows the possibility. Best part is, there is still a lot of scope for online stores expansion.

The profits of Amazon sellers

Usually when a seller starts on Amazon, the profits are not there, they will only be covering your initial capital, in terms or product selection, marketing, etc. you have to be prepared for it. Once it starts you will see a profit of at least 10%. More than 60% of sellers on Amazon have a profit margin more than 20%. This is very much achievable, make sure you are on top of the game.

Get the right product, source, marketing. Then follow up and make sure customer experience is good. The cycle has to be repeated, better not to slip which will take lot of effort to get back on pace again.

What Amazon sellers have really earned?

There are more than 35% of sellers on Amazon, who have earned more than $25000 (Around 18 lakh rupees). The top 2% of Amazon sellers have earned around $10 Million (70 crore rupees). Around 40% of people earn less than $25000. The aim should be to increase the quality and presence on Amazon. The only limit is your capability to scale and maintain the quality while doing so.

Your time commitment required on Amazon

For this, first consider how much time would you require to spend if it were a brick-and-mortar store, that you are starting up. It will be more than 10 hours per day. Around 60-70 hours per week.

Here usually first-time sellers, around 60% of them spend less than 20 hours per week on setting up the shop, that is, around 3 to 4 hours per day. Around 15% of new sellers spend less than an hour per day of week to setup and get profitable. So, it could be anywhere from 1 hours to 4 hours per day for majority of new sellers. Around 5% of the sellers end up spending almost the same time as in brick-and-mortar store (10 hours per day).

Best thing is first spending some time studying, then verify if you understanding is good enough, remember it will not be perfect, even the top sellers will have room for improvement. Once you have a good enough understanding and able to identify the good and bad sellers on Amazon by yourself, without having to buy their product to find out, you can get started confidently.

Is the new era of 2021 still suitable for Amazon selling?

With the new normal in 2021 also, there is no change seen for online sales. There is only growth possible for this mode of business. Though, there will be lot more sellers getting on to Amazon, the number consumers and the products consumed is projected be growing.

The other aspect is of competition from similar platforms which can come up. Though, that is possible, the entry barrier is huge compared to the reach and capability of Amazon. There are so many vendors or sellers on this network, along with buyers, it will take a lot of capital to provide any offer to lure the customers to another platform. Definitely no small or medium player can try that easily.

The best suggestions from existing sellers

There have been lot of people who have tried and will be trying out in future also. Many of the successful sellers, more the 50% of them say, they feel that they should have started earlier. Since the time they were thinking about starting but didn't, all seems to really wasted time.

The main suggestion is start ASAP.

It usually takes around 6 weeks to get the shop up and running.

Important things to know for staring up

✓ Nothing is perfect, just get started.
✓ It will only get more competitive as time passes by. It goes by the saying, "The best time to plant a tree was 10 years ago, now is the next best time".
✓ Research before jumping in, at least understand what it takes and what to start with.

My story and first-hand learnings

Stock market

Stock market is one of the best examples of hugely technology driven massive financial instrument. Each and every trading day, so much of money is on the line, it's mind boggling. Especially the intraday, and that too with margins, every second matters. Everything is online with millions of people dealing from various platforms, there are all possible combinations of latest technology, huge money and absolutely stringent time constraints, rules and regulations.

I have been on the market for over 15 years now in total, that includes 3 stints. Currently on the 3rd one, and this time, have finally got my complete strategy sorted out. There is so much of learning required, I sometimes think, this much of a learning curve, doesn't really match the rewards, to be specific "potential reward".

The other way of looking at it, is very simple this is a very strict environment, where there is no excuse for mistakes. You just have to learn the lesson for sure, and adhere to it, no matter what. The important part is, there are so many different kinds of pitfalls, yet just very few lessons, if properly learnt and followed, it will all be fine. The maturity of not answering any enticement is the key. Though the traps come in very convincing disguises, control of one's own Greed and Fear, takes care of everything. It is easier said than done, though.

How to earn meaningful money?

One of the famous saying in stock market is the 90-90-90 rule.

"90% of traders lose 90% of their money in the first 90 days"

This is also referred to as the stock market fees by some. It's difficult for people to learn lessons, especially build good habits. Surprisingly, people do not learn the lesson, even if it might cost them their life. Simple example is people warned of over-eating, smoking or drinking, when they are already on the brink of collapse, people won't stop drinking in spite of the last warning from Doctor. The paradigm in their mind is programmed as such, though they might very well agree and start off doing what they thought of doing, but lose track, put in other words, paradigm takes control and soon they are back doing the same old things again.

This is where the Stock market is a very strict teacher. She just rewards phenomenally, and punishes as much strictly.

I will describe my experiences for example in the stock market. I had started playing in the market more than 15 years ago, in 2004. Playing! I'll just clarify that first. Yes, everything you do is just a play, no matter how serious you think it is, or it matters. Basically, you are just wearing a hat and playing accordingly. At that time, I was just an enthusiastic investor trying to learn and earn with a mindset of "I'm a novice, will try small and see what happens, how it works?" Exactly at that time there were lot of other people who were damn serious and playing with a hat of "I have to make a living out of this, will see if I could make a fortune out of it, I have so much experience in this now".

Basically, the point is, you play according to the hat you choose to wear. There would have been many people who would have entered the market with the same level of experience as mine, but wearing a different hat, which would have made a lot of difference in the results and the experience.

Now, getting back to my stints, the first two were as a lazy trader, though at that time I thought I was investing. The first one stopped, when I had very little time to spend, and the activity didn't seem to be rewarding enough. Though some of the small investments of that time has turned good. The second time, I started after around 9 years and this time, found that there are lot of study materials and courses available for learning how to play in the stock market.

There are so many, that it gets hard to find the good ones. Best is to get started with big names and get trained. I did with some good paid ones from OTA (Online Trading Academy), which was in collaboration with a top broker in India. Though there are lot of free resources available, simple tricks in the way they give suggestions will make you feel it is very good. Only when the market turns around or does a correction, or shows some short coverings and dips, everything starts to get clarified. It's all about strategy and personal trading and investing plan. There might be a hundred things happening around, and you will still know where you are going.

This is such a big monster, and so many people and really big entities involved, that it many times affects its own cause, the companies. Not getting into too much of adjective and adverbs to talk of this, it suffices to say, it is huge and tremendously powerful. If you learn your way through, using a strategy built up on your emotions, you will do fantastic.

After having done a few courses and also having seen positive results for some time, I was confident that I will make it through the markets this time. Had two strategies one for investment and the other for trading. Basically, trading is required for two purposes, one to build capital and the other if you want regular (almost) income. With all this I was able to make decent money in trading and for investment I kept 20% of the capital.

After trading the stocks in cash segment, I started on the Futures and Options, which a derivative market it seemed to be fantastic. It went on very well for 2 months. I won twice certificates of being successful trader for 60 days in a row. I was doing this with underlying asset of equity, which was fine. Then thought, should be trying the next level, with index and weekly expiries, this is really aggressive, and realized can only be done with full attention to the market. There is no margin for error, absolutely none. Obviously, when I said I learnt, it means that I had to pay for the small gaps in attention and activeness. The fees paid was all that I earned over 6 months. Good part is the strategy helped me to stop the losses, before it could start disabling my trading activity, and best part is, the strategy got strengthened. Now, I have arrived at my strategy, which looks like the one I can use for as long as I need.

There are so many learnings, starting from generic ones such as, "once you see a streak of stop losses, stop trading a few sessions", to "Stick to your setup as much as you stuck to it while on winning streak". Still the ones that come out your trading journal are the ones which will give you lot more clarity, since they are based on Your trading profile and strategy.

There are very simple strategies, that could be built for yourself, and use that particular setup which you have whetted out and are comfortable with. You could refine this further, with a planned and experimental capital, to make sure it is up to the mark all the time. A combination of EMA, RSI, MACD, Bollinger, Support and Resistance, and Trend lines will be enough.

The learnings from stock market could be leveraged, as with any learning of value and which is in demand, using the Money Genies.

As of now I have used these Money Genies to make a meaningful earning, which are:

Money Genies used:
1. YouTube
    For learning the basics.
2. Google
    For study and research.
3. Amazon
    For buying books.

The logical next step is to use these Money Genies to leverage the learning:

Money Genies to be further used:

1. YouTube
2. OnMyGoal.com
3. Facebook Ads.
4. Amazon for selling books.

How to earn meaningful money?

I have already discussed the way each of these Money Genies could be invoked in the earlier lesson.

Udemy

The other Money Genie used is in Education. Created just one online tutorial uploaded. The tutorial is a set of videos explaining the required concepts, each of around 15 minutes of duration. The complete tutorial is around 5 hours of training. Each of the videos took more than 10 hours of recording and editing time. There was no much preparation time since it was known subject from school time. Just the conversion effort took around 50 hours for over a month.

To begin with, a sample video of a lesson was uploaded for review on Udemy. Once this was approved with their comments, I decided overview of content for the entire tutorial. Then, added all the lessons and descriptions for each of them. Also included exercises which the student will be using to check the learning. There is online help on the site to help in format of video lessons and the exercises that could be provided to students.

Once the lessons are ready, an introductory video is required, which will be shown to potential students. Make sure you take time and clearly brief, about what is covered in the course. I did this once, then after review I updated with more precise and simple description of exactly what I was teaching in the entire course.

Once done there are some lessons, which could be allowed for preview, so that student is sure that the teaching style including audio and video quality and accent, everything is acceptable to him or her. This helps the potential student to make the decision faster and with confidence.

After all this effort, the online course pretty much goes on auto-pilot. There is Question & Answer section, where a student enrolled in your course could ask any question, just answer the queries from students.

Since, there is no provision to interact with the students live, practically there is no time constraint from the instructor. So, this brings it very close to being a passive income. The only disadvantage is, the popularity of course is subjective. One way to keep it going is to continue adding lessons and also do your own marketing for the course uploaded. Even with this, there is no guarantee that student landing on the site will enroll in your course. He or She might as well land on the site, because of your Ad expense, and choose the same kind of course from another instructor.

Even with this there is an almost fully passive income of $10 (Rs. 700) per month happening now. This is, just with whatever was already known, and not trying to increase the student engagement or any Ads or promotion being done.

There are people on this platform, who have uploaded many tutorials and actively engaging with students, with marketing from their own Ad revenue and social media. These instructors earn much more than what I have mentioned above.

One simple thing you could do is to, check the website for top sold courses. On these find the number of students enrolled, this is mentioned in each course, then multiply it with the course fee. You should be reducing the number students by 20% or so. This is required since some aggressive instructors offer their course initially for free to increase the reach and get some good feedback. So, if the number of students enrolled are 10,000 and the course fee is $5, which is low, it's a revenue of around $50k. There will be around 60-70% of charges and marketing fee, so a profit of $20k (Rs. 14,00,000/-) over a period of 2 years is very much possible.

Money Genies used:
1. Udemy

Further enhancement could be done using:
1. YouTube
2. Facebook

For advertising

The Dynamics

At the time of writing this book, the Mega Robots and the numbers or these Genies are very much relevant. Yet, all these things are very dynamic and keep changing, usually growing, and many newer things keep coming up. So, I have created the portal **www.moneygenies.com** to keep track of all the latest and greatest developments happen around, for earning money. You will find lot of resources and updates on newer methods and tools captured there.

There is also a mastermind group discussing on how to use these tools, including the newer ones that keep coming, and sharing the results to help each other grow as Genie Master! Get connected.

https://www.instagram.com/moneygenies
https://twitter.com/moneygenies
https://www.facebook.com/groups/moneygenies

This is basically a practical book, helping you to master the art of using Money Genies! Reading the book is the starting point and the awareness gained from it half the work already done. Next step is to take action and taking massive action to make this a reality in your life. This is not some theoretical thing which I came up with or dreamt of. There are people, right now earning millions of dollars, that is crores of rupee, while they sitting in a beach or sleeping or doing anything else. There are these Money Genies which are working for them and depositing money in their account, whether they are enjoying, resting or working on their next interesting thing!

I would strongly encourage you to immediately join the groups which teach you how to leverage technology to free up time in your life! Doesn't matter which of them you follow, make sure you do.

5. 2+ income sources

Unless you build 2+ income sources, you will never have a comfortable vacation. Unless you build two plus income sources, you will never have a comfortable life, or vacation. Every rich person happens have more than seven sources of income. So, that's how wealth is generated. Usually, people end up running some trade or inheriting some business and continue doing the same thing throughout the life without giving any attention to other methods of earning. Any disruptions that happen, potential, technological, economical, creates a lot of risk to the business. It is dangerous and riskier to be unaware of what is happening around. You have to be on par with the latest and greatest technologies so that you can jump around and survive, to get over situations even when the whole trade is gone. The changes can come in some form, either by new technology or with new government policies or by some totally unexpected thing like a pandemic, which has happened to the modern world.

Though we are saying that we have the most innovative things possible on Earth in this era, the kinds of which, humankind has never seen before with AI and machine learning, and we are targeting the moon, we are picking up stones from the moon, and thinking of mining the moon, a pandemic shook everything. Many business and people were totally stuck because of this.

Even with this kind of disruption we should be able to, not only survive, but also thrive.

First, we will look at how people get into whatever they have. Usually, the middle class which is a majority of the population, is also the one which is vulnerable to many of these events. The other set of people in this category are the 9-5 workers. These are the ones who have gone through 14-16 years of education and then got a job at some corporate or some start-up company. Then have worked for years continuously to get ahead in the job. They at some point get another degree, maybe studying part time for the one year or so, and then continue on corporate world. If you look at it this model, he or she has already spent 14 to 16 years of continuous study without any breaks, consuming their parent's money, put in years of continuous work once again without any meaningful break.

With all this income is generated every month. In spite of having done all the work, pay will happen only when you work the whole month. Maybe they will give a month of vacation, a paid vacation, otherwise you will be paid only when you work, it doesn't matter how much you have struggled how many years your work, effort you have put, but that is not going to get paid.

Think about it, how much of this you might be able to repeat if the whole profession changes are some new things comes. Unless it is only incremental, which you can learn in jump on, it is not possible. For this reason alone, you should be preparing a second source of income.

While trying to acquire a trade or professional skill for additional income, you should try to leverage on you existing skills. The simplest of them is to train people. You could also provide a service by using the same skill, if it is feasible and, whenever there is free time. This will make sure that you will be able to leverage to a great extent by putting in two hours of work. Just by two or three hours every day, or maybe 10 to 12 hours per week, you should be able to double your income. This is the smallest thing that you could do when you build two plus income sources.

Now what happens if any major disruption came in, you'll be able to at least survive for the sometime and be able to jump on to another job, or learn another skill peacefully with the buffer, which you have built. This is very important and is actually being used by many people. They are always on the edge trying to learn new things and be ready to jump on the new thing, because they know the new things are always coming.

Some examples you can think of are the people who have really jumped off using the Udemy courses. There are many who started it as a hobby and found it started working out, and generating meaningful money. Then, they put in some more effort and the effect of being global showed up and could clearly see the revenues started exceeding the salary they were earning after more than 20-25 years (16 of Education + 5-10 years or work) or preparation. Not, that all the education and experience has gone waste, but it is being leveraged to its best capability. They have just extended their services far beyond their physical presence and capability. Capability? Yes, the courses run 24/7, you can't do anything 24/7 for 365 days a year. These technologies do it for you. You could just focus on the real expertise of solving and answering key questions, which your clients get. I'm just bringing this emphatically to your Attention! Just so that you learn to invoke a Money Genie for yourself!

6. Express your Passion

Make sure to express your passion, to get career satisfaction. The next commandment which you should employ is, "unless you express your passion, you will never get career satisfaction." There are only few people who live the life they were born to live. Basically, career forms major part of your meaningful life, when you have Energy, Money and Time. If you are not careful or watchful enough you will work just for money and lose the most precious thing you have, the life.

Career is not just a corporate job, political position, bureaucratic post, it is the way you make most of your living from. It could be farming, an independent service, art, whichever skill or service people have paid you for.

Everyone has a career, no matter what they do, unless until you are totally living out of your parent's money and or somebody else's money and you have done no work, and nobody has ever paid you for anything. This I assume as pretty rare. Clearly, having career in not a choice but how good or bad, Is.

I have already described the logical way of categorizing professions, as either primary, secondary, and tertiary. These help in identifying how quick or feasible is it to make your passion as your career, in the society you are in. Just to give a very rough example, if your passion is Music and you are in a place, where people are struggling to keep themselves out of huger, your chances of making a comfortable living out from your passion, becomes really challenging, and you might have to consider moving to a more conducive place.

Now a look at the occupations' categories according to Wikipedia:

1. Primary,
2. Secondary, and
3. Tertiary.

Start of Wikipedia reference…

Primary

The primary sector of the economy includes any industry involved in the extraction and production of raw materials, such as farming, logging, hunting, fishing, and mining.

The primary sector tends to make up a larger portion of the economy in developing countries than it does in developed countries. For example, in 2018, agriculture, forestry, and fishing comprised more than 15% of GDP in Sub-Saharan Africa but less than 1% of GDP in North America.

In developed countries the primary sector has become more technologically advanced, enabling for example the mechanization of farming, as compared with hand-picking and -planting in poorer countries. More developed economies may invest additional capital in primary means of production: for example, in the United States corn belt, combine harvesters pick the corn, and sprayers spray large amounts of insecticides, herbicides and fungicides, producing a higher yield than is possible using less capital-intensive techniques. These technological advances and investment allow the primary sector to employ a smaller workforce, so developed countries tend to have a smaller percentage of their workforce involved in primary activities, instead having a higher percentage involved in the secondary and tertiary sectors.

Secondary

In macroeconomics, the secondary sector of the economy is an economic sector in the three-sector theory which describes the role of manufacturing. It encompasses the industries which produce a finished, usable product or are involved in construction.

This sector generally takes the output of the primary sector (i.e. raw materials) and creates finished goods suitable for use by other businesses, for export, or for sale to domestic consumers (via distribution through the tertiary sector). Many of these industries consume large quantities of energy and require factories and machinery; they are often classified as light or heavy based on such quantities. They also produce waste materials and waste heat that may cause environmental problems or cause pollution (see negative externalities). Examples include textile production, car manufacturing, and handicraft.

Manufacturing is an important activity in promoting economic growth and development. Nations that export manufactured products tend to generate higher marginal

GDP growth which supports higher incomes and marginal tax revenue needed to fund quality-of-life initiatives such as health care and infrastructure in the economy. The field is an important source for engineering job opportunities. Among developed countries, it is an important source of well-paying jobs for the middle class to facilitate greater social mobility for successive generations on the economy. Currently, an estimated 20% of the labour force in the United States is involved in the secondary industry.

The secondary sector depends on the primary sector for the raw materials necessary for production. Countries that rely on agriculture and other raw materials i.e. (primary sector), grow slowly and remain under-developed or developing economies. The value addition after the processing of goods creates for higher profitability, which accounts for the growth of developed economies.

Tertiary

The tertiary sector of the economy, generally known as the service sector, is the third of the three economic sectors of the three-sector theory. The others are the secondary sector (approximately the same as manufacturing), and the primary sector (raw materials).

The service sector consists of the production of services instead of end products. Services (also known as "intangible goods") include attention, advice, access, experience, and affective labour. The production of information has been long regarded as a service, but some economists now attribute it to a fourth sector, the quaternary sector.

The tertiary sector of industry involves the provision of services to other businesses as well as final consumers. Services may involve the transport, distribution and sale of goods from producer to a consumer, as may happen in wholesaling and retailing, pest control or entertainment. The goods may be transformed in the process of providing the service, as happens in the restaurant industry. However, the focus is on people by interacting with people and serving the customer rather than transforming the physical goods

...End of Wikipedia reference.

Make sure that your career is able to express your passion as much as possible so that your performance soars.

Working just for making money will not be able sustainable for a long time. You have to make sure that, when you are waking up in the morning you just jump out of bed to start working. That is a clear measure and indication of whether you are working on your passion or not.

This state of yourself will also have direct implication on your physical and mental health. We have seen many people who are seem to be very successful by all measures of wealth, income and their lifestyle, but not really happy. Obviously, they are not working out of their passion. It only means they are trying to impress people around with their life style and wealth, but ignoring to impress themselves. Their own self, the real passion is dying within them, but they are not able to help it out.

Pay close attention to this (I assume you are paying attention all through, just that I want to make absolutely sure that, some very key observation skills, you should not miss learning from this book), When you see someone is working hard two things are possible. These two things are kind of opposites, basically showing up as, the same hard work as seen from external point of view. This could be happening for two diametrically opposite reasons. When you see someone working hard, just ask the question, Is the person doing that out of Compulsion or out of Choice.

Anyone stretching themselves due to compulsions would be deteriorating, while the person stretching out of choice will be strengthening. This choice must be the internal one, not the one where people are trying to impress others. So, unless you are really observant and haven't built experience in clearly seeing, both kind of hard work will seem the same.

It's becoming kind of overkill, yet I think it is better to clarify little more, so that there is no ambiguity with this key point. If a person is jumping out of bed and starts working for many weeks or months in a row, and you start thinking he is working out passion, might not be watch closely, the act of jumping out bed to work itself should not be the pride of the person. Whenever, he has accomplished a milestone, he should be rejoicing, relaxing, and he or she gets back up on the path of goal.

If he or she is just doing it for impressing people around, it would not work, and you will see he or she is in fact destroying his or her health. On the other hand, the same thing is happening and the only pride of the person is the accomplishment, and he does take a break, a vacation, however small or big, he is working out of choice. So, the key distinction is, person while on the working-hard cycle will be happy about it, just like

Arnold says, people in the gym around him used ask him, "we are also working 5-6 hours a day but how is that you have a smile on your face." The answer is Choice.

7. Skill for Financial Confidence

Only way to be financially confident is to develop a skill in demand using your free time. Everyone has Financial confidence, the only question is how strong or weak it is, or if it's even negative.

Financial confidence is the measure of clarity and belief you have in earning a living and thrive over a period of time, irrespective of your staring point.

Basically, with financial confidence you are not just sure about the wealth and physical assets you have, but about the skills which you have used to acquire them. So, obviously for person relying totally upon inherited wealth, might be very less, in spite being rich, unless he or she has acquired the multiplying skills.

It's about the fishing skills you have learnt along the way, not just the number of fishes you have right now. As we have discussed earlier in the Primary, Secondary and Tertiary occupations, you should identify the kind of occupation which is thriving around you. Your passion should be falling in one of the categories of occupation.

List and choose a skill which you will be able to acquire with minimal effort in line with your passion and hone it.

Sometimes, the skillset which is in high demand, in your environment would also be the one which aligns to your passion. Then, it becomes lot easier to develop the skill and skyrocket your financial confidence.

The key point is, whether your passion fully aligns with the demand or not, you should find the intersection of your passion and in-demand skillset and develop it. This will build the confidence which percolates into all other areas of life.

This also helps in following your passion and taking decisions, knowing clearly that you have skill to survive any eventuality and no one can flatten you. You can clearly stand your ground.

Keep it as a hobby, this will be such a booster, you wouldn't believe how it works out. Usually, people have many skillsets, just that not all of them could be commercialized or converted into income sources, because you are not focussing. For example, an engineer, doctor, artist who know multiple languages, which doesn't seem much, but there are people making money just with multiple languages as translators, as voice over artists, as teachers.

You might be a teacher, lawyer, mechanic, who knows how to cook, which again might not seem much at the first look. Just check out how money people are making on YouTube showing the recipes, they are preparing delicious food enjoy cooking it, then relish it on camera and getting paid for it, sometime in 1000s of dollars every month, or just being a cook. Any skillset is useful in this era, the only limitation is which you have somehow come up with. Those were just some examples of skillsets, to make the point, which people usually ignore. You could find many more easily, just look for it.

Leverage the technology and monetize your skill or interest. There are various ways you could come up with to work on the areas of you interest of passion always. For example, if you are good at mathematics and clearly visualize and enjoy the number, there relationships to each other, how they play out on graph, how numbers are all around in nature, this could be hard for some people. With this you could of course be an accountant with straight forward known tasks, or invest in stock market diving into to the deep ocean of technical analysis, if you don't like the risk and emotional quotient required, just teach the techniques and you could be making as much money as you want.

So, from cooking, to drawing, to language skills, to mathematics, almost anything, could be monetized leveraging today's technology, the Money Genies!

All the limitations you see are the ones which you have created for yourself. Just dump them and just,

Invoke the Money Genies!

-They work 24x7 for you.

Notes